쓰담
쓰담
내신영문법

3

장재영

유명 어학원과 영어학원에서 강의하면서 강사, 부원장, 원장을 역임.
(전) 리딩스타어학원 디렉터
(전) 청담어학원 원장
(전) 아발론교육 원장
(현) 고려대학교 국제어학원 영어교육프로그램 EiE 원장
특목고 진로 컨설팅
저서 「제대로 영작문」 시리즈

지은이 장재영
펴낸이 정규도
펴낸곳 (주)다락원

초판 1쇄 발행 2017년 1월 5일
초판 2쇄 발행 2018년 7월 26일

편집 김민주, 김미경, 이동호
디자인 구수정
영문 감수 Michael A. Putlack
삽화 박하
조판 블랙 엔 화이트

다락원 경기도 파주시 문발로 211
내용문의 (02)736-2031 내선 502
구입문의 (02)736-2031 내선 250~252

Fax (02)732-2037
출판등록 1977년 9월 16일 제406-2008-000007호

Copyright © 2017 장재영

값 11,000원

ISBN 978-89-277-0797-4 54740
　　　978-89-277-0794-3 54740(set)

http://www.darakwon.co.kr

다락원 홈페이지를 방문하시면 상세한 출판정보와 함께
동영상강좌, MP3 자료 등 다양한 어학 정보를 얻으실 수 있습니다.

쓰담
쓰담
내신영문법

3

이 책의 구성과 특징

핵심만 간추린 중요 문법 사항으로 문법의 기초를 다지고
서술형 위주로 엄선한 최신 기출 응용 문제로 내신 시험에 대비합니다.

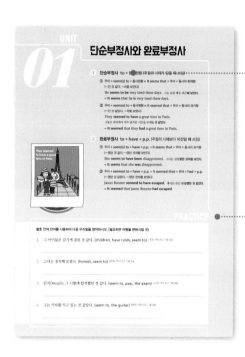

핵심 문법 사항

중3 수준에서 반드시 알아야 할 중요 문법 사항들의 핵심만 간추려 정리했습니다.

PRACTICE

간단한 문장을 영작하면서 위에서 학습한
문법 사항을 점검해 봅니다.

연습문제는 모두 기출 응용 문제로 구성되어 있습니다.

NOW REAL TEST ①
기출 응용 문제

7~10문항으로 구성된 최신 기출 응용 문제로
중학 내신 시험의 출제 경향을 파악할 수 있습니다.

서술형 문제 위주로 구성되어 있어,
학생들이 어려워하는 서술형 문제에
대비할 수 있습니다.

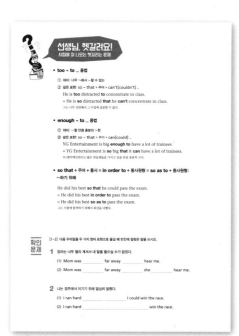

NOW **REAL TEST** ❷
실전 예상 문제

3~6문항으로 구성된 실전 예상 문제로 내신 시험에
본격적으로 대비합니다.

서술형 문제 위주로 구성되어 있어, 학생들이
어려워하는 서술형 문제에 대비할 수 있습니다.

선생님, 헷갈려요!
시험에 잘 나오는 헷갈리는 문제

학생들이 잘 모르거나 헷갈려 하는 문법 사항, 구동사,
관용 표현 등을 짚고 넘어가는 코너입니다.

특히 시험에 잘 나오는 항목으로 엄선하여 내신 시험에
효과적으로 대비합니다.

차례

Chapter 1 to부정사

UNIT 01 단순부정사와 완료부정사	010
UNIT 02 가주어, 가목적어 it	016
선생님, 헷갈려요! to ~ to … 용법 / enough ~ to … 용법 / so that + 주어 + 동사	022

Chapter 2 관계사

UNIT 03 관계대명사	024
UNIT 04 관계부사	029
선생님, 헷갈려요! 관계부사와 「전치사 + 관계대명사」의 사용	034

Chapter 3 완료형, 수동태, 비교 구문

UNIT 05 완료형	036
UNIT 06 수동태, 비교 구문	041
선생님, 헷갈려요! by 이외의 전치사를 쓰는 수동태	046

Chapter 4 조동사, 간접의문문

UNIT 07 조동사	048
UNIT 08 간접의문문	053
선생님, 헷갈려요! 주의해야 할 조동사 표현	058

Chapter 5 접속사

UNIT 09 접속사 that, 등위 접속사	060
UNIT 10 부사절을 이끄는 접속사	066
선생님, 헷갈려요! 헷갈리기 쉬운 접속사 관련 표현	072

Chapter 6 분사구문

UNIT 11 분사구문의 의미 ——————————————— 074
UNIT 12 주의해야 할 분사구문 ————————————— 079

선생님, 헷갈려요! 의문사 + to부정사 ———————— 084

Chapter 7 가정법

UNIT 13 가정법 과거 ————————————————— 086
UNIT 14 가정법 과거완료 —————————————— 091

선생님, 헷갈려요! 사역동사: ～하게 하다 —————— 096

Chapter 8 화법과 일치

UNIT 15 화법(1) ——————————————————— 098
UNIT 16 화법(2), 일치 ———————————————— 103

선생님, 헷갈려요! It is said that: ～라고 말해진다 —— 108

Chapter 9 강조, 도치, 동격

UNIT 17 강조 ———————————————————— 110
UNIT 18 도치와 동격 ———————————————— 115

선생님, 헷갈려요! 여러 가지 부정 표현 ——————— 120

Chapter

1

to부정사

UNIT 01   단순부정사와 완료부정사

UNIT 02   가주어, 가목적어 it

UNIT 01 단순부정사와 완료부정사

1 단순부정사 to + 동사원형 (주절과 시제가 같을 때 쓰임)

① 주어 + seem(s) to + 동사원형 = It seems that + 주어 + 동사의 현재형
(~인 것 같다, ~처럼 보인다)
He **seems to be** very tired these days. 그는 요즘 매우 피곤해 **보인다.**
= **It seems** that he **is** very tired these days.

② 주어 + seemed to + 동사원형 = It seemed that + 주어 + 동사의 과거형
(~인 것 같았다, ~처럼 보였다)
They **seemed to have** a great time in Paris.
그들은 파리에서 아주 즐거운 시간을 보내는 **것 같았다.**
= **It seemed** that they **had** a great time in Paris.

2 완료부정사 to + have + p.p. (주절의 시제보다 이전일 때 쓰임)

① 주어 + seem(s) to + have + p.p. = It seems that + 주어 + 동사의 과거형
(~였던 것 같다, ~였던 것처럼 보인다)
She **seems to have been** disappointed. 그녀는 실망했던 것처럼 보인다.
= **It seems** that she **was** disappointed.

② 주어 + seemed to + have + p.p. = It seemed that + 주어 + had + p.p.
(~였던 것 같았다, ~였던 것처럼 보였다)
Jason Bourne **seemed to have escaped.** 제이슨 본은 탈출했던 것 같았다.
= **It seemed** that Jason Bourne **had escaped.**

PRACTICE

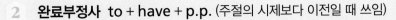

괄호 안의 단어를 사용하여 다음 우리말을 영작하시오. (필요하면 어형을 변화시킬 것)

1 그 아이들은 감기에 걸린 것 같다. (children, have colds, seem to) 난우중 3학년 최근 기출 응용

_____

2 그녀는 정직해 보였다. (honest, seem to) 금옥중 3학년 최근 기출 응용

_____

3 민지(Minji)는 그 시험에 합격했던 것 같다. (seem to, pass, the exam) 강신중 3학년 최근 기출 응용

_____

4 그는 기타를 치고 있는 것 같았다. (seem to, the guitar) 원촌중 3학년 최근 기출 응용

_____

NOW REAL TEST ①

1 괄호 안에 주어진 단어를 사용하여 다음 우리말을 영작하시오. 광장중 3학년 최근 기출 응용

그는 좋은 작곡가인 것 같다. (it, a good songwriter)

→ _____

2 주어진 문장과 의미가 같도록 빈칸을 채우시오. 중앙중 3학년 최근 기출 응용

It seems that Tom and Jerry are scared.

→ Tom and Jerry _____ _____ _____ _____ .

3 다음 문장을 의미의 변화 없이 Inguk을 주어로 한 seem to ~ 구문으로 고쳐 쓰시오. 동덕여중 3학년 최근 기출 응용

It seems that Inguk got enough rest for his next role.

→ Inguk _____ .

4 두 문장의 의미가 같도록 빈칸 ⓐ, ⓑ에 알맞은 말이 순서대로 짝지어진 것은? 기안중 3학년 최근 기출 응용

It _____ ⓐ _____ that they bought the house for a good price.
= They seem to _____ ⓑ _____ the house for a good price.

	ⓐ		ⓑ
①	seems	–	buy
②	seems	–	bought
③	seems	–	have bought
④	seemed	–	buy
⑤	seemed	–	have bought

NEW WORDS

☐ **songwriter** 작곡가 ☐ **scared** 겁 먹은 ☐ **role** 역할, 배역 ☐ **for a good price** 괜찮은 가격에

5 다음 그림의 상황을 두 가지 현재 시제 문장으로 나타낼 때, 빈칸에 알맞은 말을 쓰시오.
(반드시 seem을 사용하고 필요할 경우 어형을 바꿀 것) 가락중 3학년 최근 기출 응용

(1) It _____ .

(2) The boy _____ .

6 다음 밑줄 친 (가)와 바꿔 쓸 수 있는 표현으로 가장 적절한 것은? 광주진흥중 3학년 최근 기출 응용

> While he was talking to Dongryong, Jeonghwan noticed that Dongryong wasn't paying attention. Instead, (가) it seemed that he was looking at the wall behind Jeonghwan.

① it seemed to look at the wall
② he seemed to look at the wall
③ he seemed to be looking at the wall
④ it seemed to be looking at the wall
⑤ he seemed to looking at the wall

7 주어진 문장과 같은 의미가 되도록 문장을 완성하시오. 광희중 3학년 최근 기출 응용

(1) She seemed to be upset.

　　→ It _____ .

(2) It seems that they knew the truth at that time.

　　→ They _____ .

NEW WORDS

☐ **notice** 알아차리다　☐ **pay attention** 주의를 기울이다　☐ **instead** 그 대신에　☐ **upset** 속상한　☐ **truth** 진실
☐ **at that time** 당시에

8 다음 중 어법상 <u>어색한</u> 문장은? 고양제일중 3학년 최근 기출 응용

① It seemed that he is a good teacher.

② He seems to have a lot of cameras.

③ It seems that they exercise every day.

④ Jasmine seemed to have arrived there on time.

⑤ It seemed that he could pass the test.

9 주어진 문장을 It seems that ~ 또는 It seemed that ~ 구문으로 바꾸어 쓰시오. 원곡중 3학년 최근 기출 응용

(1) JYP seems to be a creative company.

→ _____

(2) Edison seemed to be a genius.

→ _____

10 주어진 문장을 「주어 + seem(s) to + 동사원형」으로 바꾸어 쓰시오. 원곡중 3학년 최근 기출 응용

(1) It seems that Sujin takes good care of her younger brother.

→ _____

(2) It seems that Jongguk drove very well in the dark.

→ _____

NEW WORDS

☐ **on time** 제시간에   ☐ **creative** 창의적인   ☐ **genius** 천재   ☐ **take good care of** ~을 잘 돌보다

NOW REAL TEST ❷

1 다음 중 어법에 맞지 <u>않는</u> 문장을 찾아 바르게 고쳐 쓰시오.

ⓐ The man seems to be a dentist.

ⓑ He seemed to have finished it.

ⓒ She seemed that she was a pianist.

→ _____

[2-3] 다음 대화의 밑줄 친 부분과 의미가 같도록 빈칸에 알맞은 말을 쓰시오.

2

A Have you ever seen a ghost?

B Yes, I have. <u>It seems that ghosts are real.</u>

→ Ghosts seem _____ .

3

A Look. Her name is not on the invitation list.

B I'm sorry. <u>It seems that one of our staff members made a mistake.</u>

→ One of our staff members seems _____ .

NEW WORDS

□ **dentist** 치과 의사 □ **ghost** 유령 □ **invitation** 초대 □ **staff member** 직원 □ **mistake** 실수

4 다음은 찬미가 영어 공부를 하다가 쓴 오답노트이다. 세 항목 중 설명이 <u>잘못된</u> 것을 골라 번호를 쓰시오.

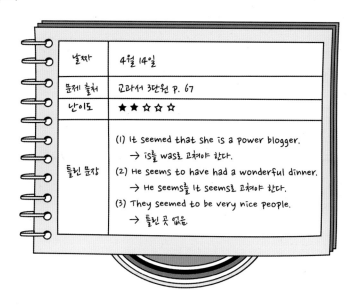

날짜	4월 14일
문제 출처	교과서 3단원 P. 67
난이도	★ ★ ☆ ☆ ☆
틀린 문장	(1) It seemed that she is a power blogger. → is를 was로 고쳐야 한다. (2) He seems to have had a wonderful dinner. → He seems를 It seems로 고쳐야 한다. (3) They seemed to be very nice people. → 틀린 곳 없음.

→ _____

5 다음 우리말을 두 가지 영어 문장으로 완성하시오.

그녀는 어제 거기 없었던 것 같다.

(1) It seems _____.

(2) She seems _____.

NEW WORDS

☐ **power blogger** 영향력이 큰 블로그(blog)를 운영하는 사람

UNIT 02

가주어, 가목적어 it

1 **가주어, 가목적어 it**

주어나 목적어가 to부정사구 혹은 that절처럼 긴 경우, 가주어나 가목적어로 it을 사용한다.

2 **it ~ to부정사**

① 가주어

To understand your explanation is very hard.

→ **It** is very hard **to understand** your explanation.

② 가목적어

We found **it** difficult **to forgive** the criminals.

우리는 그 범죄자들을 용서하는 것이 어렵다고 생각했다.

3 **It ~ that + 주어 + 동사**

① 가주어

That she broke up with James is shocking.

→ **It** is shocking **that she broke up** with James.

② 가목적어

I find **it** strange **that he got** an A⁺ on the test.

나는 그가 그 시험에서 A⁺를 받았다는 것을 이상하게 생각한다.

4 **의미상 주어**

① 일반적인 경우: **for + 목적격**

It is hard **for me** to exercise for over two hours a day.

② 사람의 성품·성질을 나타내는 형용사(nice, kind, foolish, wise, polite, rude, careless, brave 등)가 있을 경우: **of + 목적격**

It is very nice **of him** to donate a lot of money to charity.

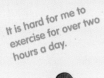

It is hard for me to exercise for over two hours a day.

PRACTICE

괄호 안의 단어를 사용하여 다음 우리말을 영작하시오.

1 그 기자가 진실을 밝힌 것은 용감했다. (it, brave, reveal the truth, reporter, to) _{백신중 3학년 최근 기출 응용}

_____

2 너희가 영어를 배우는 것은 매우 중요하다. (learn, important, it, to) _{반포중 3학년 최근 기출 응용}

_____

3 네가 나를 도운 것은 친절했다. (kind, it, to) _{대왕중 3학년 최근 기출 응용}

_____

4 그가 아직도 돌아오지 않았다는 것은 이상하다. (it, strange, that, back) _{대화중 3학년 최근 기출 응용}

_____

NOW REAL TEST ❶

1 주어진 표현을 사용하여 〈조건〉에 맞게 문장을 쓰시오. 행신중 3학년 최근 기출 응용

> 〈조건1〉 가주어 It, 진주어 to부정사 사용할 것
>
> 〈조건2〉 현재 시제로 쓸 것

(1) dangerous, me, swim, in the deep river

→ _____

(2) kind, you, let me know, this information

→ _____

2 괄호 안에서 필요한 단어만 사용하여 우리말 의미에 맞는 영어 문장을 완성하시오. 주곡중 3학년 최근 기출 응용

(1) 우리가 이 상자들을 옮기는 것은 어렵지 않다. (carry, for, to, these, boxes, of, us)

→ It isn't difficult _____.

(2) 네가 그 컵을 깨뜨린 것은 조심성이 없었다. (break, the, cup, of, for, to, you)

→ It was careless _____.

3 밑줄 친 부분이 어법상 올바른 것은? 송라중 3학년 최근 기출 응용

① It is very kind of him to say that.
② It is very easy of her to solve the question.
③ It is impossible of us to finish the project this week.
④ Is it okay for our to stay a little longer?
⑤ It is nice for you to help the poor.

4 빈칸에 들어갈 말이 나머지와 다른 하나는? 송호중 3학년 최근 기출 응용

① It is dangerous _____ the children to enter the haunted house.
② It is boring _____ us to watch the drama on TV.
③ It was stupid _____ you to believe such a thing.
④ It is hard _____ me to build a cage without any help.
⑤ It was not easy _____ me to lose weight.

NEW WORDS

☐ **careless** 부주의한　☐ **impossible** 불가능한　☐ **haunted** 귀신이 나오는　☐ **cage** 새장, 우리

5 다음 그림을 보고, 주어진 표현을 활용하여 문장을 완성하시오.
(It ~ to 구문을 사용하고 의미상 주어를 사용할 것) 이목중 3학년 최근 기출 응용

Eric

(watch TV, until late at night, not good)

→ _____

6 〈보기〉에서 알맞은 단어를 골라 〈조건〉에 맞게 영어 문장을 완성하시오. 내동중 3학년 최근 기출 응용

〈조건 1〉 단어는 한 번씩만 쓸 것

〈조건 2〉 각 빈칸에 하나의 단어만 쓸 것

〈보기〉 you, for, of, me

(1) I asked my homeroom teacher, "Is it okay _____ _____ to skip the homework?"

(2) I told him, "It is kind _____ _____ to pick me up."

7 다음 중 어법상 틀린 것은? 도농중 3학년 최근 기출 응용

① It's important of you to exercise regularly.

② It was nice of him to do such a good thing.

③ It is very difficult for Jane to memorize it just in an hour.

④ It was generous of her to accept the proposal.

⑤ It's not easy for us to speak in English.

NEW WORDS

☐ **skip** 빠뜨리다, 거르다　☐ **pick up** ~을 태워주다　☐ **regularly** 규칙적으로　☐ **memorize** 암기하다

☐ **generous** 너그러운　☐ **accept** 받아들이다　☐ **proposal** 제안

8 주어진 우리말을 다음 세 가지 〈조건〉에 맞게 영어로 쓰시오. _{성사중 3학년 최근 기출 응용}

〈조건 1〉 주어와 동사를 갖춘 완전한 문장으로 쓸 것

〈조건 2〉 9단어로 쓸 것

〈조건 3〉 It으로 문장을 시작할 것

미란(Miran)이가 그 제안을 거절한 것은 현명했다. (wise, refuse, offer)

→ _____

9 다음 글을 읽고, 밑줄 친 부분을 어법에 맞게 고쳐 쓰고, 우리말로 해석하시오. _{원곡중 3학년 최근 기출 응용}

Two years ago, Yura had only one dog. But now, there are six dogs and five cats in her house. All of them were stray animals. Her friends often say to her, "It's very nice for you look after stray animals."

(1) 어법에 맞게 고쳐 쓰시오.

→ _____

(2) 우리말로 해석하시오.

→ _____

10 다음 두 문장을 It을 사용하여 한 문장으로 만드시오. _{반송중 3학년 최근 기출 응용}

〈조건〉 괄호 안의 두 단어를 반드시 사용할 것

(1) Kevin wears a helmet when inline skating. It is safe. (safe, to)

→ _____

(2) Inpyo caught a robber. He was brave. (brave, to)

→ _____

NEW WORDS

☐ **refuse** 거절하다 ☐ **offer** 제안 ☐ **stray** 길 잃은 ☐ **look after** ~을 돌보다 ☐ **inline skate** 인라인 스케이트를 타다
☐ **robber** 강도

1 다음 우리말을 두 가지 표현으로 영작할 때, 빈칸에 알맞은 말을 쓰시오.

네가 너만의 좌우명을 가지는 것은 매우 좋다.

(1) It is very good _____ _____ _____ have your own motto.

(2) It is very good _____ you have your own motto.

2 다음 빈칸에 알맞은 말이 순서대로 짝지어진 것은?

- It's easy _____ to learn how to play the guitar.
- It's very smart _____ to solve it so quickly.
- It was impossible _____ to read two books a day.

① for me – for her – of him
② for her – of you – for him
③ of you – for him – for you
④ of her – for her – for him
⑤ for me – of her – of him

3 주어진 단어를 사용하여 다음 문장을 It으로 시작하는 문장으로 쓰시오.

(1) Zidane led Real Madrid. (exciting)

→ _____

(2) Enrique encouraged his players in spite of their faults. (generous)

→ _____

NEW WORDS

☐ **motto** 좌우명 ☐ **encourage** 격려하다 ☐ **in spite of** ~에도 불구하고 ☐ **fault** 잘못 ☐ **generous** 너그러운, 관대한

4 다음 글의 밑줄 친 ⓐ를 〈보기〉의 단어를 활용하여 영어로 쓰시오. (필요하면 어형을 바꿀 것)

My family went to Italy last winter. We didn't stay at a hotel but stayed in a local house which we had booked on a room-sharing website. ⓐ (우리에게는 그 곳에 머무르는 것이 훨씬 더 저렴했다.) Moreover, we had a good experience with the host family.

〈보기〉 it, to, stay, for, we, much, cheap, there

→ _____

5 다음 대화의 흐름에 맞도록 괄호 안에 주어진 단어를 활용하여 빈칸을 완성하시오. (주어진 단어 외에 추가로 필요한 단어를 더 써야 함)

Jacob   I'm sorry, Tina.

Tina   You are late again. What happened?

Jacob   As you know, I had a big baseball game.

Tina   I understand, but _____.

(important, it, for, to, on, time, be, you)

NEW WORDS

☐ **local** 지역의   ☐ **book** 예약하다   ☐ **share** 공유하다   ☐ **moreover** 게다가   ☐ **experience** 경험   ☐ **host** 주인
☐ **happen** 일어나다

- ## too ~ to ... 용법

  ① 의미: 너무 ~해서 …할 수 없는

  ② 같은 표현: so ~ that + 주어 + can't[couldn't] ...

  He is **too** distracted **to** concentrate in class.

  = He is **so** distracted **that** he **can't** concentrate in class.

  그는 너무 산만해서 그 수업에 집중할 수 없다.

- ## enough ~ to ... 용법

  ① 의미: …할 만큼 충분히 ~한

  ② 같은 표현: so ~ that + 주어 + can[could] ...

  YG Entertainment is big **enough to** have a lot of trainees.

  = YG Entertainment is **so** big **that** it **can** have a lot of trainees.

  YG엔터테인먼트는 많은 연습생들을 가지고 있을 만큼 충분히 크다.

- ## so that + 주어 + 동사 = in order to + 동사원형 = so as to + 동사원형: ~하기 위해

  He did his best **so that** he could pass the exam.

  = He did his best **in order to** pass the exam.

  = He did his best **so as to** pass the exam.

  그는 시험에 합격하기 위해서 최선을 다했다.

확인문제

[1-2] 다음 우리말을 두 가지 영어 표현으로 옮길 때 빈칸에 알맞은 말을 쓰시오.

1 엄마는 너무 멀리 계셔서 내 말을 들으실 수가 없었다.

(1) Mom was _____ far away _____ hear me.

(2) Mom was _____ far away _____ she _____ hear me.

2 나는 경주에서 이기기 위해 열심히 달렸다.

(1) I ran hard _____ I could win the race.

(2) I ran hard _____ win the race.

Chapter

2

관계사

UNIT 03   관계대명사

UNIT 04   관계부사

03

관계대명사

1 관계대명사의 계속적 용법

① 선행사에 대한 부가적인 설명으로, 관계대명사 앞의 절부터 해석한다.

② 선행사 다음에 콤마(,)를 붙인다.

③ 「접속사(and, but, because 등) + 대명사」로 바꿀 수 있다.

I met my old friend, **who** is now a police officer.

= I met my old friend, **and he** is now a police officer.

나는 옛 친구를 만났는데, 그는 지금 경찰관이다.

④ 계속적 용법의 which는 앞 문장의 일부나 문장 전체를 받는다.

I bought these apples, **which** were grown on an organic farm.

= I bought these apples because they were grown on an organic farm. 나는 이 사과들을 샀는데, 유기농 농장에서 재배되었기 때문이다.

The boys laughed at a beggar, **which** annoyed me.

그 소년들은 거지를 비웃었는데, 그것은 나를 짜증나게 했다.

⑤ 관계대명사 that과 what은 계속적 용법으로 쓰지 않는다.

I bought a new bike, **that** was on sale. (×)

I bought these apples, which were grown on an organic farm.

2 관계대명사 what = the thing(s) that / the thing(s) which

I know **what** you did last summer. 나는 네가 지난 여름에 한 일을 알고 있다.

3 관계대명사의 생략

① 목적격 관계대명사의 생략

The woman (**whom**) I met yesterday is my music teacher.

② 주격 관계대명사 + be동사

Do you know the boy (**who is**) sitting on the bench?

PRACTICE

괄호 안의 단어를 사용하여 다음 우리말을 영작하시오.

1 나는 사촌이 한 명 있는데, 그는 일본으로 공부하러 갔다. (cousin, who) 송산중 3학년 최근 기출 응용

_____

2 나는 오빠가 하나 있는데, 그는 변호사이다. (lawyer, who) 경민여중 3학년 최근 기출 응용

_____

와동중 3학년 최근 기출 응용

3 내가 너희에게 질문을 하나 할 건데, 그것은 대답하기 어려워. (ask, question, answer, which)

_____

4 그 도둑이 그 집에서 찾은 것은 작은 반지였다. (what, thief, found, ring) 언북중 3학년 최근 기출 응용

_____

NOW **REAL TEST** ❶

1 다음 대화를 완성하시오. <small>양천중 3학년 최근 기출 응용</small>

    A Is this the car that they need?

    B Yes, this is just ＿＿＿＿＿＿＿ ＿＿＿＿＿＿＿ need.

2 다음 대화에서 B가 한 말을 관계대명사 what을 사용하여 다시 쓰시오. <small>상촌중 3학년 최근 기출 응용</small>

    A Did Becky tell us the truth?

    B Well, I think it's a lie.

  → I think ＿＿＿＿＿＿＿＿＿＿＿＿＿＿＿＿＿＿.

3 다음 두 문장을 관계대명사의 계속적 용법을 사용하여 한 문장으로 만드시오. <small>원곡중 3학년 최근 기출 응용</small>

(1) He said nothing. It made me angry.

    → ＿＿＿＿＿＿＿＿＿＿＿＿＿＿＿＿＿＿

(2) Simon hates hot weather. Hot weather makes him tired.

    → ＿＿＿＿＿＿＿＿＿＿＿＿＿＿＿＿＿＿

4 다음 그림을 보고, 관계대명사 what을 사용하여 대화의 빈칸에 알맞은 말을 쓰시오. <small>마전중 3학년 최근 기출 응용</small>

    W Is this the new smartphone that you want to have?

    M Yes, this is ＿＿＿＿＿＿＿＿＿＿＿＿.

5 괄호 안의 단어를 사용하여 우리말을 영어로 옮기시오. (필요하면 단어를 추가하거나 변형할 것)

(1) 이것은 내가 정말 원했던 것이 아니다. (is, what, this, not, I, want)

→ _____

(2) Joy가 원하는 것은 자유다. (freedom, want, what, is)

→ _____

6 계속적 용법의 관계대명사를 사용하여 다음 문장을 다시 쓰시오.

(1) Here is some water, and it is very cold.

→ _____

(2) I know the woman, and Jason danced with her last Saturday.

→ _____

7 주어진 질문에 대한 답을 〈조건〉에 맞게 쓰시오.

〈조건 1〉 완전한 영어 문장으로 쓸 것

〈조건 2〉 관계대명사 what을 사용할 것

〈의미〉 내가 저녁으로 먹고 싶은 것은 파스타(pasta)이다.

Q **What do you want to eat for dinner?**

A _____

8 관계대명사 what을 사용하여 다음 두 문장을 한 문장으로 바꾸어 쓰시오.

My father cooked something for us yesterday, and it was really delicious.

→ _____ **was really delicious.**

NEW WORDS

☐ **freedom** 자유

1 다음 두 문장을 한 문장으로 만들 때, 빈칸에 알맞은 말을 <u>5단어</u>로 쓰시오.

- My sister is sick.
- It makes my family worried.

→ My sister's sickness is _____ .

2 연우는 존경하는 인물을 세종대왕으로 정했고, 그분에 대한 특별한 것은 한글을 창제했다는 점이라고 말하려고 한다. 주어진 〈조건〉에 맞게 문장을 완성하시오.

〈조건 1〉 다음 표현을 반드시 사용할 것

(what, special about him, that, invented Hangeul)

〈조건 2〉 주어와 동사를 포함한 완전한 문장으로 쓸 것

→ The person that I admire is King Sejong. I think that _____

_____ .

3 밑줄 친 <u>What[what]</u>의 용법이 〈보기〉와 같은 것은?

〈보기〉 This is <u>what</u> I want to buy.

① Can you tell me <u>what</u> your name is?
② <u>What</u> she wants to do now is play games.
③ Do you know <u>what</u> this is?
④ <u>What</u> a good car this is!
⑤ I wonder <u>what</u> she wore at the party.

NEW WORDS

☐ **worried** 걱정하는 ☐ **sickness** 병 ☐ **admire** 존경하다 ☐ **invent** 창제하다, 발명하다

4 다음 중 어법상 틀린 문장은?

① What my father wants me to do is study hard.

② I have two sons, who are teachers.

③ He knows what we did last night.

④ I bought a new cell phone, that is really cool.

⑤ What I really want to do is eat ice cream.

5 David가 생일에 원하는 것을 나타낸 다음 표를 보고, 관계대명사 what을 사용하여 빈칸을 채우시오. (David가 말하는 것처럼 쓸 것)

하고 싶은 일	친구들과 점심 먹기
선물로 받고 싶은 것	새 자전거
저녁 식사로 먹고 싶은 것	스테이크

(1) _____ on my birthday is to have lunch with my friends.

(2) _____ for my birthday present is a new bike.

(3) _____ for dinner is steak.

관계부사

1 관계부사

「접속사 + 부사」의 역할을 하고 선행사를 수식한다. 「전치사 + 관계대명사」로 바꿀 수 있다.

① when: 선행사가 시간(the day, the time 등)을 나타낼 때 (= in/at/on which)

This is the day. My brother passed the test on the day.

→ This is the day **when** my brother passed the test. (= on which)

② where: 선행사가 장소(the place, the city 등)를 나타낼 때 (= in/at/on/to which)

I visited the city. Bill Gates was born in the city.

→ I visited the city **where** Bill Gates was born. (= in which)

③ why: 선행사가 이유(the reason)일 때 (= for which)

He told me the reason. He wore white clothes for the reason.

→ He told me the reason **why** he wore white clothes. (= for which)

④ how: 선행사가 the way일 때 *단, how와 the way는 반드시 둘 중 하나만 써야 한다.

I will tell you the way. I overcome crises in the way.

→ I will tell you **the way** I overcome crises. (= how / the way in which)

He told me the reason why he wore white clothes.

2 복합관계사

① 복합관계대명사

whoever: 누구든지 (= anyone who, no matter who)

whichever: 어느 것이든지 (= anything that, no matter which)

whatever: 무엇이든지 (= anything that, no matter what)

② 복합관계형용사: whatever + 명사 (어떤 ~라도), whichever + 명사 (어느 ~라도)

③ 복합관계부사

whenever: ~할 때마다, 언제 ~하더라도 (= at any time, no matter when)

wherever: ~하는 곳마다, 어디서 ~하더라도 (= at any place, no matter where)

however: 아무리 ~하더라도 (= no matter how)

PRACTICE

괄호 안의 단어를 사용하여 다음 우리말을 영작하시오. (관계부사를 사용하고, 필요하면 어형을 변화시킬 것)

1 Amy는 자기 아버지가 가르치시는 학교에 다닌다. (go to the school, where) 동성중 3학년 최근 기출 응용

_____

2 너는 수지(Suji)가 화난 이유를 아니? (angry, the reason) 덕산중 3학년 최근 기출 응용

_____

3 그녀가 그 식물들을 창문 앞에 두었던 이유를 말해 줘. (plants, the reason, in front of, put) 금옥중 3학년 최근 기출 응용

_____

4 그는 그 빵집에 들를 때마다 많은 빵을 산다. (stop by, bakery, a lot of) 남대문중 3학년 최근 기출 응용

_____

NOW REAL TEST ①

1　우리말과 같은 뜻이 되도록 where를 사용하여 영어 문장을 완성하시오. <small>일산동중 3학년 최근 기출 응용</small>

그들이 자란 집은 아름다운 바다 전망을 가지고 있었다.

→ The house _____ a beautiful view of the sea.

2　다음 중 빈칸에 들어갈 말이 차례대로 짝지어진 것은? <small>상동중 3학년 최근 기출 응용</small>

  A　Do you know the reason _____ people usually put candles in the bedroom?

  B　Well, I place them in the bedroom because it is the place _____ I spend the most time.

  ① why – when　　　② when – why　　　③ why – which

  ④ why – where　　　⑤ that – which

3　다음 그림에 어울리도록 주어진 단어를 배열하여 엄마가 하신 말씀을 완성하시오. <small>상하중 3학년 최근 기출 응용</small>

→ Do you know _____ ?

(why, I, scolding, am, you, the, reason)

NEW WORDS

☐ **view** 전망　☐ **candle** 양초　☐ **scold** 야단치다, 꾸짖다

4 빈칸에 적절한 관계부사를 쓰시오. 김포중 3학년 최근 기출 응용

(1) Do you know the reason _____ she came here?

(2) A library is a place _____ people can find various books.

(3) Do you remember the time _____ you finished your project?

(4) The house _____ Michael Jackson lived was very luxurious.

5 다음 주어진 두 문장을 한 문장으로 만들 때 어법상 <u>어색한</u> 것은? 광무여중 3학년 최근 기출 응용

He remembered the day. He first met her on that day.

① He remembered the day which he first met her.

② He remembered the day when he first met her.

③ He remembered the day on which he first met her.

④ He remembered the day which he first met her on.

⑤ He remembered the day that he first met her on.

6 다음 문장과 의미가 같도록 빈칸을 채우시오. 대덕중 3학년 최근 기출 응용

However busy you are, don't forget to send an email to your teacher.

→ _____ _____ _____ _____ _____ , don't

forget to send an email to your teacher.

7 다음 문장과 의미가 같도록 주어진 단어를 사용하여 문장을 완성하시오. 탄방중 3학년 최근 기출 응용

(1) No matter which bike you choose, I'll buy it for you. (whichever)

→ I will buy you _____ .

(2) However well you drive, you must not drive too fast. (no matter)

→ _____ , you must not drive

too fast.

NEW WORDS

☐ **various** 다양한 ☐ **luxurious** 호화로운

1 다음 문장에서 어법상 <u>어색한</u> 곳을 찾아 바르게 고쳐 쓰시오.

This is the hotel in where many famous entertainers stay.

_____ → _____

2 다음 빈칸에 들어갈 말이 차례대로 짝지어진 것은?

• Saturday is the day _____ we meet to study English.

• This restaurant is the place _____ I had a nice dinner with her.

① when – how ② which – where ③ when – which

④ on which – where ⑤ which – in which

3 다음 우리말과 같은 의미의 두 문장을 쓸 때, 빈칸에 알맞은 말을 쓰시오.

그 차가 아무리 비싸더라도, Mansour는 그것을 살 것이다.

(1) _____ expensive the car may be, Mansour will buy it.

(2) _____ _____ _____ expensive the car may be, Mansour will buy it.

4 다음 표를 보고, 빈칸에 알맞은 말을 쓰시오.

구입일	지난주 토요일
구입처	명동에 있는 Darak Shoes
구입 이유	신발을 잃어버려서

(1) Last Saturday was the day _____ Jack _____ new shoes.

(2) Darak Shoes in Myeongdong is the store _____ Jack _____ them.

(3) The reason _____ Jack _____ them was that he had lost his old shoes.

NEW WORDS

☐ entertainer 연예인

5 다음은 승우의 일기 중 일부이다. 〈보기〉에서 알맞은 단어를 골라 일기를 완성하시오.

〈보기〉 day   why   when   reason   where

   I am a soccer player in Korea. I want to go to England to play in the Premier League, ⓐ _____ I can meet great soccer players. I want to play soccer with them. That's the ⓑ _____ ⓒ _____ I've studied English hard. I think Son Heungmin's and Ki Sungyueng's success in England comes not only from their soccer skills but also from their fluent English. Yesterday was the ⓓ _____ ⓔ _____ the tryouts began. I really want to go to England.

6 다음 그림을 보고, 〈조건〉에 맞게 빈칸을 채우시오.

〈조건〉 시간을 나타내는 관계부사를 사용할 것

   Tomorrow is _____ _____ _____ summer vacation starts. I want to go to my grandparents' house in the countryside. I can swim and fish there. I will get up early tomorrow.

NEW WORDS

☐ **success** 성공 ☐ **skill** 기술 ☐ **fluent** 유창한 ☐ **tryout** 입단 테스트 ☐ **countryside** 시골

● 관계부사와 「전치사 + 관계대명사」의 사용

when: in/at/on which

March 1 is the day **when** I was born.

3월 1일은 내가 태어난 날이다.

= March 1 is the day **on which** I was born.

= March 1 is the day **which** I was born **on**.

= March 1 is the day **that** I was born.

= March 1 is the day **that** I was born **on**.

where: in/at/on/to which

That small church is the place **where** James first met Sally.

저 작은 교회는 James가 Sally를 처음 만났던 장소이다.

= That small church is the place **at which** James first met Sally.

= That small church is the place **which** James first met Sally **at**.

= That small church is the place **that** James first met Sally.

= That small church is the place **that** James first met Sally **at**.

why: for which

I don't know the reason **why** she doesn't like him.

나는 그녀가 그를 좋아하지 않는 이유를 모르겠다.

= I don't know the reason **for which** she doesn't like him.

= I don't know the reason **which** she doesn't like him **for**.

= I don't know the reason **that** she doesn't like him.

= I don't know the reason **that** she doesn't like him **for**.

확인 문제

다음 우리말과 의미가 같도록 빈칸에 알맞은 말을 쓰시오.

> 그것이 그가 그녀에게 사실을 말하지 않았던 이유이다.

(1) That is the reason _____ he didn't tell her the truth.

(2) That is the reason _____ he didn't tell her the truth.

(3) That is the reason _____ he didn't tell her the truth _____.

(4) That is the reason _____ he didn't tell her the truth.

(5) That is the reason _____ he didn't tell her the truth _____.

Chapter

3

완료형, 수동태, 비교 구문

UNIT 05   완료형

UNIT 06   수동태, 비교 구문

UNIT 05 완료형

1 현재완료 진행

① 쓰임: 과거에 시작되어 현재에도 계속 진행 중인 일을 나타낼 때 사용

② 형태: have[has] been + -ing (~해 오고 있는 중이다)

He started to play games this morning. He's still playing games.

→ He **has been playing** games since this morning.

그는 오늘 아침부터 게임을 **해 오고 있는 중이다.**

2 과거완료(대과거)

① 쓰임: 과거보다 이전에 일어난 일을 나타낼 때 사용

② 형태: had p.p.

When the policeman arrived, the thief **had** already **left.**

경찰이 도착했을 때, 도둑은 이미 **떠났었다.** (경찰 도착: 과거, 도둑이 떠남: 대과거)

3 과거완료 진행

① 쓰임: 과거보다 이전에 시작되어 과거의 어느 시점까지 계속 진행 중인 일을 나타낼 때 사용

② 형태: had been + -ing (~해 오고 있던 중이었다)

He was sleeping there. Then, they came.

→ He **had been sleeping** there when they came.

그들이 왔을 때 그는 거기서 **자고 있었던 중이었다.**

When the policeman arrived, the thief had already left.

4 미래완료

① 쓰임: 미래의 어떤 시점까지 완료, 지속될 것으로 예상되는 일을 나타낼 때 사용

② 형태: will have p.p. (~하게 될 것이다, ~한 셈이 된다)

I **will have lived** in Seoul for 15 years next year.

내년이면 나는 서울에 15년 동안 **산 것이 된다.**

PRACTICE

괄호 안의 단어를 사용하여 다음 우리말을 영작하시오. (필요하면 어형을 변화시킬 것)

1 그녀는 3년 동안 우리에게 음악을 가르쳐 오고 있다. (teach us, for) 신동중 3학년 최근 기출 응용

_____

수서중 3학년 최근 기출 응용
2 성경은 오랫동안 사람들에게 교훈을 주고 있다. (the Bible, give, lessons, for a long time)

_____

3 그녀는 30분 동안 그 노래를 듣고 있는 중이다. (listen to, for) 문정중 3학년 최근 기출 응용

_____

송호중 3학년 최근 기출 응용
4 우리가 극장에 도착했을 때, 그 영화는 벌써 시작했었다. (theater, get to, begin, when, already)

_____

NOW REAL TEST ①

1 다음 두 문장을 한 문장으로 연결할 때, 빈칸에 알맞은 말을 쓰시오. 양정중 3학년 최근 기출 응용

He began to play the guitar three hours ago. He is still playing the guitar.

→ He _____ _____ _____ the guitar _____ three hours.

2 우리말 뜻에 맞게 두 문장을 연결하시오. (단, 반드시 두 사건의 순서가 나타나도록 할 것) 성내중 3학년 최근 기출 응용

She went out. I stopped by her house. (내가 그녀의 집을 들렀을 때, 그녀는 외출했었다.)

→ _____

3 다음 대화를 읽고, 빈칸에 알맞은 말을 쓰시오. (주어진 단어를 모두 사용하되, 필요하면 어형을 변화시킬 것) 대왕중 3학년 최근 기출 응용

A Wow! Hyerin, you are good at dancing.
B Thank you. But I am still learning.
A How long have you been learning?
B I _____. (have, be, learn, a year, for)

4 〈보기〉에서 알맞은 단어를 골라 빈칸에 적절한 형태로 쓰시오. 신남중 3학년 최근 기출 응용

〈보기〉 get   buy   leave   eat

(1) The train _____ _____ when I _____ to the station.

(2) I _____ another hamburger for my younger brother because my cousin _____ _____ all the hamburgers.

NEW WORDS

☐ **still** 아직도 ☐ **stop by** ~에 들르다 ☐ **station** 역

5 괄호 안의 단어를 어법에 맞게 변형 및 배열하여 빈칸에 알맞은 문장을 쓰시오. _{덕현중 3학년 최근 기출 응용}

I overslept this morning. I had to run to school. _____,
_____. (get, start, already, to, I, school,
when, the class, have) As a result, I had to clean the restroom.

6 다음 대화를 읽고, 대화 내용을 요약할 수 있는 문장을 〈조건〉에 맞게 완성하시오. _{동암중 3학년 최근 기출 응용}

〈조건 1〉 괄호 안의 단어를 사용할 것

〈조건 2〉 주어진 상황에 맞는 시제를 사용할 것

Mom   Jerry, come out here. What are you doing?

Jerry   I am playing *Overwatch*!

Mom   You started playing it an hour ago. Are you still playing it?

→ Jerry _____. (play, an hour, for)

7 다음 중 어법상 <u>어색한</u> 문장은? _{장성중 3학년 최근 기출 응용}

① I had never met her before then.

② He said that he had called her a few times before.

③ I bought a new bag because I have lost my old one.

④ When they got home, they found somebody had broken the window.

⑤ He had already left the airport when his mom arrived.

8 다음 대화를 읽고, 괄호 안의 단어를 바르게 배열하여 빈칸을 채우시오. _{별망중 3학년 최근 기출 응용}

A   I want to show you something.

B   What is it?

A   This is a special stamp that my grandfather bought 60 years ago. Even my
father wasn't born at that time.

B   You're saying this is a stamp that _____
_____? (your grandfather, before, had, your father, bought, was, born)

NEW WORDS

☐ **as a result** 그 결과로   ☐ **restroom** 화장실

NOW REAL TEST ❷

1 다음 두 문장을 한 문장으로 만드시오.

My father started to wash his car this morning. He is still washing it.

→ _____

2 우리말과 같은 뜻이 되도록 현재완료 진행형을 사용하여 문장을 완성하시오.

(1) 그녀는 세 시간 동안 TV를 보고 있다.

→ She has _____ _____ TV for three hours.

(2) Louise는 오늘 아침부터 쇼핑을 하고 있다.

→ Louise has _____ _____ since this morning.

3 다음 그림을 보고, 시간의 순서와 어법에 맞게 문장을 완성하시오. (단, 현재 시각은 6시임)

Jack   Henry

〈조건 1〉 괄호 안의 단어를 사용할 것

〈조건 2〉 어형을 알맞게 변화시킬 것

When Henry _____ _____ at 5 o'clock, Jack _____

already _____ the chicken. (come home, eat)

4 다음은 Jamie의 오후 계획표이다. 빈칸에 알맞은 말을 쓰시오. (단, 현재 시각은 오후 2시임)

12:00 – 1:00	Have Lunch
1:00 – 4:00	Study English
4:00 – 5:00	Get Some Rest

(1) Jamie _____ _____ English for an hour.

(2) At 4 p.m., Jamie _____ _____ studying English. He will get some rest after that.

5 오늘은 8월 1일이다. 다음 지유(Jiyu)의 일정표를 보고, 미래완료 시제를 사용하여 문장을 완성하시오.

August 2	Leave for Jeju
August 3	Climb Halla Mountain
August 4	Come Back to Daegu

By August 5,

(1) Jiyu _____ Halla Mountain.

(2) Jiyu _____ back to Daegu.

NEW WORDS

☐ **climb** 등반하다

UNIT 06

수동태, 비교 구문

① 수동태

① 현재형: am/are/is p.p.

Is this seat **taken**? 이 자리 주인이 있나요?

② 과거형: was/were p.p.

My room **was cleaned** by my mom. 내 방은 엄마에 의해 **청소되었다.**

③ 미래형: will be p.p.

This guitar **will be played** by the musician.
이 기타는 그 음악가에 의해 **연주될 것이다.**

④ 조동사의 수동태: 조동사 + be p.p.

The policy **should be followed**. 그 정책은 **이행되어야 한다.**

⑤ 진행형의 수동태: be동사 + being p.p.

This building **is being built** by many people.
이 건물은 많은 사람들에 의해 **지어지고 있다.**

⑥ 완료형의 수동태: have/has been p.p.

A lot of money **has been donated** to Africa by him.
많은 돈이 그에 의해 아프리카로 **기부되어 왔다.**

② 비교 구문

① the + 비교급 ~, the + 비교급 …: ~하면 할수록 더 …한

The more people have, **the more** they want.
사람들은 더 **많이** 가지면 가질**수록** 더 **많이** 원한다.

② 비교급 + and + 비교급: 점점 더 ~한

The game is getting **more and more exciting**.
경기가 **점점 더 흥미진진해지고 있다.**

Is this seat taken?

괄호 안의 단어를 사용하여 다음 우리말을 수동태 문장으로 영작하시오. (필요하면 어형을 변화시킬 것)

1 그 신발은 짚신(*jipsin*)이라고 불려진다. (shoes, call) 목일중 3학년 최근 기출 응용

_____

2 그 가방은 Mark에 의해 버려질지도 모른다. (throw away, may) 부천남중 3학년 최근 기출 응용

_____

3 그 아기는 1년 동안 Sylvia에 의해 보살핌을 받아 왔다. (for, take care of, have) 문정중 3학년 최근 기출 응용

_____

4 우리는 나이가 들면 들수록 더 현명해진다. (the, get, wise, become) 진건중 3학년 최근 기출 응용

_____

NOW REAL TEST ❶

1 다음 우리말을 〈조건〉에 맞게 영작하시오. _{송라중 3학년 최근 기출 응용}

〈조건 1〉 「the + 비교급 ~, the + 비교급 …」을 사용할 것

〈조건 2〉 주어진 단어를 사용하되, 필요한 경우에는 단어를 추가하거나 변형할 것

네가 더 열심히 공부하면 할수록 더 높은 점수를 받을 것이다. (hard, study, high, score, get)

→ _____

2 다음 글의 내용을 〈조건〉에 맞게 한 문장으로 표현할 때, 빈칸에 알맞은 말을 쓰시오. _{가원중 3학년 최근 기출 응용}

〈조건〉 현재완료 수동태 문장으로 완성할 것

Sam began to memorize the words on Monday. It's Friday today. He is still memorizing them.

→ **The words** _____ .

3 다음 대화를 읽고, 밑줄 친 우리말을 〈조건〉에 맞게 영작하시오. _{목일중 3학년 최근 기출 응용}

〈조건 1〉 괄호 안에 주어진 단어를 모두 사용할 것

〈조건 2〉 새로운 단어를 추가할 수 없음

〈조건 3〉 필요하면 단어의 형태를 바꿀 것

A I have a lot of Spanish homework. Do you know anyone who can help me?

B Oh, Emily can speak Spanish. Her Spanish friend Silvia taught her.

A Really? 그녀는 얼마나 오랫동안 Silvia에게 가르침을 받았니? (have, been, teach, by, how long, she, Silvia)

B For more than three years.

→ _____

NEW WORDS

☐ **score** 점수 ☐ **Spanish** 스페인어; 스페인의, 스페인 사람의

4 다음 문장의 밑줄 친 부분이 <u>틀렸으면</u> 맞게 고쳐 쓰고, 맞으면 그대로 다시 쓰시오. _{민락중 3학년 최근 기출 응용}

The more books you read, <u>detailed</u> information you will get.
(너희가 더 많은 책을 읽을수록, 더 자세한 정보를 얻게 될 것이다.)

→ _____

5 다음 문장을 같은 의미의 수동태 구문으로 바꾸어 쓰시오. _{개운중 3학년 최근 기출 응용}

Koreans have loved *bulgogi* for a long time.

→ _____

6 괄호 안의 단어를 사용하여 〈조건〉에 맞게 다음 우리말을 영작하시오. _{망포중 3학년 최근 기출 응용}

〈조건1〉 「the + 비교급 ~, the + 비교급 …」을 사용할 것
〈조건2〉 어법에 맞는 완전한 문장을 쓸 것

눈이 더 많이 올수록, 아이들은 더 많은 눈사람을 만든다. (it, heavily, snowmen)

→ _____

7 밑줄 친 (가)를 어순에 맞게 배열하시오. _{행신중 3학년 최근 기출 응용}

This container can hold 100 liters of water, and it (가) (should, wheel, be, rolled, a, like). It is our company's main product for this summer.

→ _____

NEW WORDS

□ **detailed** 자세한 □ **snowman** 눈사람 □ **container** 용기 □ **liter** 리터 □ **wheel** 바퀴 □ **main** 주된
□ **product** 상품

8 적절한 시제를 사용하여 대화의 흐름에 맞게 빈칸을 채우시오. 신동중 3학년 최근 기출 응용

현석　Hey, what are you doing?

진영　I am writing a song for a new idol group.

현석　When did you start writing it?

진영　I started at 2 o'clock.

현석　It's 6:05 now. Then the song ＿＿＿＿＿ ＿＿＿＿＿ ＿＿＿＿＿ for more than four hours! I hope it's going to be a fantastic song.

세마중 3학년 최근 기출 응용

9 다음 그림의 내용을 나타내는 문장을 주어진 단어를 사용하여 〈조건〉에 맞게 영작하시오.

〈조건 1〉　'~하면 할수록 더 …한'의 의미로 쓸 것

〈조건 2〉　필요하면 단어를 추가하거나 주어진 단어의 어형을 변화시킬 것

(high, we, go up, cold, it, become)

→ ＿＿＿＿＿＿＿＿＿＿＿＿＿＿＿＿＿＿＿＿＿＿

10 주어진 단어를 활용하여 다음 문장의 빈칸에 알맞은 말을 쓰시오.

(필요하면 단어를 추가하거나 어형을 변화시킬 것) 상도중 3학년 최근 기출 응용

He doesn't know anything about Korean culture because he ＿＿＿＿＿

＿＿＿＿＿＿＿＿＿＿＿. (Korean, before, expose, culture, to, not, have)

NEW WORDS

☐ **fantastic** 멋진　☐ **expose** 노출시키다　☐ **culture** 문화

1　다음 대화의 밑줄 친 부분을 어법에 맞게 고쳐 쓰시오.

> A　Oh, your son is much taller than before.
>
> B　He eats a lot. He is getting <u>tall and tall</u> these days.

→ _____

2　다음 대화에서 <u>어색한</u> 부분을 찾아 그 문장을 바르게 고쳐 쓰시오.

> A　Can you tell me how I can stay healthy?
>
> B　Having good eating habits is very important. More slowly you eat, healthier you will be.

_____　→　_____

3　다음 문장을 수동태로 바꾸어 쓸 때, 빈칸에 알맞은 말을 쓰시오.

My uncle has collected old stones since 1994.

→ Old stones _____ _____ _____
my uncle since 1994.

4　다음 대화를 읽고, 괄호 안의 단어를 사용하여 어법에 맞는 문장을 완성하시오.
(필요하면 단어를 추가하거나 어형을 변화시킬 것)

> A　Congratulations! You got Lee Seungyeop's 600th home run ball!
>
> B　Thank you. How lucky I am!
>
> A　The ball _____, shouldn't it?
>
> 　　(be, keep, carefully, your, house, very, in)
>
> B　Well, I think I will donate the ball to the baseball museum.

NEW WORDS

☐ **stay healthy** 건강을 유지하다　☐ **habit** 습관　☐ **Congratulations** 축하합니다　☐ **carefully** 주의해서
☐ **donate** 기증하다

- **by** 이외의 전치사를 쓰는 수동태

be interested in	~에 흥미가 있다
be surprised at/by	~에 놀라다
be disappointed at/with/about/by	~에 실망하다
be delighted at	~에 기뻐하다
be tired of	~에 싫증 나다
be composed of	~로 구성되다
be covered with	~로 덮여 있다
be pleased with	~에 기쁘다
be filled with	~로 채워져 있다
be satisfied with	~에 만족하다
be known to	~에게 알려지다
be known as	~로서 알려지다
be known for	~로 유명하다
be worried about	~을 걱정하다
be made from	~로 만들어지다(재료 변함)
be made of	~로 만들어지다(모양만 변하고 재료 변하지 않음)

확인문제

다음 우리말과 같은 뜻이 되도록 빈칸에 알맞은 말을 쓰시오.

(1) 나의 아버지는 항상 나의 건강을 걱정하신다.

My father _____ always _____ _____ my health.

(2) 그 그림은 많은 사람들에게 알려져 있다.

The painting _____ _____ _____ many people.

(3) 그는 그의 성적에 실망하지 않았다.

He _____ not _____ _____ his grade.

Chapter

4

조동사, 간접의문문

UNIT 07   조동사

UNIT 08   간접의문문

UNIT 07 조동사

1 조동사 + have p.p.

① **must have p.p.**: ~했음이 틀림없다

He looked very pale yesterday. He **must have been** sick.

그는 어제 무척 창백해 보였다. 아팠음이 **틀림없다**.

② **should have p.p.**: ~했어야 했다(하지 못한 것에 대한 후회)

I **should have watched** the final match last night.

나는 어젯밤에 결승전 경기를 **봤어야 했다**. (못 본 것에 대한 후회)

③ **should not have p.p.**: ~하지 말았어야 했다(한 것에 대한 후회)

You **should not have eaten** ramen last night.

너는 어젯밤에 라면을 **먹지 말았어야 했어**.

④ **can't (= cannot) have p.p.**: ~했을 리가 없다

The politician **can't have received** a bribe.

그 정치인이 뇌물을 **받았을 리가 없다**.

⑤ **may[might] have p.p.**: ~했을지도 모른다

I **may have put** my key on the desk.

나는 내 열쇠를 책상 위에 **두었을지도 모른다**.

The politician can't have received the bribe.

2 그 밖의 조동사

① **would rather + 동사원형**: 차라리 ~하는 편이 낫다

I **would rather play** video games. 나는 비디오 게임을 **하는 편이 낫겠어**.

We **would rather not stay** here. 우리는 여기 머물지 않는 편이 낫겠다.

② **used to + 동사원형**: ~하곤 했다, ~이었다

She **used to go** to the hill on weekends. 그녀는 주말에 그 언덕에 **가곤 했다**.

There **used to be** a small post office at the corner.

모퉁이에 작은 우체국이 **있었다**.

PRACTICE

괄호 안의 단어를 사용하여 다음 우리말을 영작하시오.

1 그녀는 나를 잊었음이 틀림없다. (forget) 부곡중 3학년 최근 기출 응용

_____

2 그는 그 방명록에 그의 이름을 썼어야 했는데. (visitors' book, in, write, should) 안곡중 3학년 최근 기출 응용

_____

3 너는 그 콘서트 티켓을 사지 말았어야 했다. (concert ticket, buy, should) 수원제일중 3학년 최근 기출 응용

_____

4 그는 여름에 그의 친구들과 함께 여행을 하곤 했다. (used to, travel, with) 광희중 3학년 최근 기출 응용

_____

NOW REAL TEST ①

1 주어진 문장과 같은 의미가 되도록 빈칸에 알맞은 말을 쓰시오.

일신여중 3학년 최근 기출 응용

(1) There was a big rock at the center of my hometown. It does not exist now.

→ _____ _____ _____ _____ a big rock at the center of my

hometown.

(2) I am sure that the man gave his umbrella to the old woman. 서일중 3학년 최근 기출 응용

→ The man _____ _____ _____ his umbrella to the old woman.

2 다음 중 우리말과 영어 문장이 <u>잘못</u> 짝지어진 것은? 공릉중 3학년 최근 기출 응용

① 나는 그녀에게 선물을 줬어야 했는데. → I should have given a present to her.

② 그녀가 그의 사무실에 들렀던 것이 틀림없다. → She must have stopped by his office.

③ 그가 포기했을 리가 없다. → He can't have given up.

④ 너는 그녀를 믿지 말았어야 했는데. → You should have believed her.

⑤ Tom은 큰 나무 아래에서 휴식을 취하곤 했다. → Tom used to rest under the big tree.

3 다음 대화의 흐름에 맞게 빈칸에 알맞은 말을 쓰시오.
(단, 괄호 안의 표현을 사용하고 should와 have를 반드시 포함할 것) 방산중 3학년 최근 기출 응용

Jihun   What's wrong, Minho?

Minho   I stayed up late last night playing games. I'm very tired.

Jihun   Oh, no. You _____ . (go to bed, early)

Minho   I know.

무원중 3학년 최근 기출 응용

4 주어진 단어를 사용하여 대화의 흐름에 맞게 빈칸에 알맞은 말을 쓰시오. (필요하면 어형을 바꿀 것)

A   Ted looks exhausted today.

B   That's strange. He is always energetic because he eats a lot for breakfast every day.

A   Hmm... He _____ breakfast today. (have, might, skip)

NEW WORDS

☐ **exist** 존재하다   ☐ **stay up** 안 자고 깨어 있다   ☐ **exhausted** 기진맥진한   ☐ **energetic** 활동적인

5 다음 대화가 자연스럽게 이어지도록 주어진 단어를 배열하여 빈칸을 채우시오. 풍성중 3학년 최근 기출 응용

> A You are Steve, right? You have changed a lot. You _____
>
> _____. (used to, glasses, wear, before) But you aren't wearing glasses
>
> now.
>
> B You're right. I got LASIK surgery last year.

6 다음은 Charles의 일기이다. Charles에게 해 줄 수 있는 조언을 괄호 안에 주어진 단어를 사용하여 완성하시오. 관양중 3학년 최근 기출 응용

> I went to the amusement park today. The roller coaster was very exciting. When I rode it, my heart began to beat faster. At that moment, I saw Jasmine. Because of my fast heartbeat, I thought I liked her. So I told her how I felt. But now, I don't think I like her. I realized that my fast heartbeat was not because of her but because of the roller coaster. I regret telling her that I liked her.

→ You: Charles, you _____ _____ _____ twice. (think)

7 그림을 보고, 주어진 단어를 활용하여 빈칸에 알맞은 말을 쓰시오. 민락중 3학년 최근 기출 응용

> Nami locked herself out of her house. She can't open the door now. She remembers putting the key on the table. She thinks that she _____ _____ _____ the key on the table. (not, leave)

NEW WORDS

☐ **LASIK** 라식(레이저 각막 회복 수술)   ☐ **surgery** 수술   ☐ **amusement park** 놀이공원   ☐ **beat** (심장이) 뛰다
☐ **at that moment** 그때, 그 순간에   ☐ **heartbeat** 심장 박동   ☐ **realize** 깨닫다   ☐ **regret** 후회하다

8 주어진 문장과 같은 의미가 되도록 다음 문장을 완성하시오. (반드시 「조동사 + have p.p.」를 사용할 것)

(1) I'm sure he didn't make a mistake on purpose.

→ He _____ a mistake on purpose.

(2) She is sorry that she bought such an expensive bag.

→ She _____ such an expensive bag.

9 다음 글을 읽고, 엄마의 모습을 표현하는 문장을 used to를 사용하여 완성하시오.

My mom has had long hair for 15 years. Yesterday, an actress with short hair was on TV. She looked very beautiful. So my mom decided to get a haircut. Yesterday, she went to the hairdresser and got a haircut.

→ My mom _____, but now she has short hair.

NEW WORDS

☐ **on purpose** 고의로, 일부러 ☐ **actress** 여배우 ☐ **decide** 결심하다 ☐ **get a haircut** 머리를 자르다
☐ **hairdresser** 미용사

1 다음 대화의 밑줄 친 부분에서 어색한 곳을 찾아 바르게 고쳐 문장을 다시 쓰시오.

A How was the movie? I wanted to see it, but I didn't have time.

B It was fantastic! <u>You must have seen it.</u>

→ _____

2 괄호 안의 단어를 의미가 통하도록 빈칸에 배열하시오.

_____ when I was young.

(used, here, be, a, well, big, there, to)

3 다음 중 밑줄 친 used to의 쓰임이 나머지 넷과 다른 하나는?

① He <u>used to</u> play chess with Kevin.

② My grandmother <u>used to</u> make hot chocolate for me.

③ Jean is <u>used to</u> repairing cars.

④ There <u>used to</u> be many children in the park.

⑤ My brother and I <u>used to</u> fish when we were young.

4 다음 우리말을 영어로 옮길 때 빈칸에 알맞은 말을 쓰시오.

난 그런 불량식품을 먹느니 차라리 점심을 먹지 않겠다.

→ I _____ lunch than eat such junk food.

5 다음 글에서 어색한 표현을 찾아 바르게 고쳐 쓰시오.

Today, I wore my brother's new shoes without his permission. It rained suddenly in the afternoon, and the shoes got dirty. My brother will be mad at me. I shouldn't have asked him before I wore them.

→ _____

NEW WORDS

□ **well** 우물 □ **junk food** 불량식품 □ **permission** 허락 □ **suddenly** 갑자기 □ **mad at** ~에게 화가 난

08 간접의문문

1 **간접의문문** 의문문이 문장 안에서 명사절의 역할을 하는 것

2 **의문사 없는 간접의문문** whether[if] + 주어 + 동사

*if는 목적어절에서만 사용한다.

Whether[≠If] he is rich or not is not important. (주어)
그가 부자인지 아닌지는 중요하지 않다.

I don't know. + Does he like me?
→ I don't know **whether[if]** he likes me. (목적어)
나는 그가 나를 좋아하는지 모르겠다.

The question is **whether**[≠If] he will accept it or not.
문제는 그가 그것을 받아들일 것인지 아닌지이다.

3 **의문사 있는 간접의문문** 의문사 + 주어 + 동사

I don't know. + Why did he say that?
→ I don't know **why he said** that.
나는 그가 왜 그렇게 말했는지 모르겠다.

Tell me. + How much money did you spend last night?
→ Tell me **how much money you spent** last night.
어제 네가 돈을 얼마나 많이 썼는지 나한테 말해 봐.

4 **의문사가 문두에 오는 경우**

주절의 동사가 think, imagine, suppose, guess, believe 등일 경우,
의문사가 문장 맨 앞으로 온다.

Do you think? + Why do they like Korean dramas?
→ **Why do you think** they like Korean dramas?
너는 왜 그들이 한국 드라마를 좋아한다고 생각하니?

Why do you think they like Korean dramas?

PRACTICE

괄호 안의 단어를 사용하여 간접의문문을 포함하도록 다음 우리말을 영작하시오. (필요하면 어형을 변화시킬 것)

1 나는 호랑이가 토끼보다 더 빠른지 궁금하다. (whether, than, wonder) 오마중 3학년 최근 기출 응용

_____

수일중 3학년 최근 기출 응용

2 너는 너 자신에게 네가 정말 무엇을 원하는지 물어야 한다. (ask, yourself, what, really, should)

_____

3 그들은 그가 그 차를 얼마나 빨리 운전했는지 궁금해했다. (how, fast, drive, wonder) 수일중 3학년 최근 기출 응용

_____

4 너는 어제 그녀가 왜 회의에 늦었다고 생각하니? (why, the conference, late, for) 명인중 3학년 최근 기출 응용

_____

NOW REAL TEST ①

1 다음 두 문장을 간접의문문을 이용하여 한 문장으로 바꾸어 쓰시오. 상록중 3학년 최근 기출 응용

(1) Do you know? + Where is the zoo?

→ Do you know _____ ?

(2) She wants to know. + How much time does he have?

→ She wants to know _____ .

2 다음 글에서 어법상 오류를 찾아 수정한 후, 그 이유를 우리말로 쓰시오.
(단, 어법요소와 이유를 모두 쓸 것) 부천여중 3학년 최근 기출 응용

Have you ever wondered what will you do when you face the last day of the world? It's very frightening. Nobody wants to face the last day of the world.

(1) 오류: _____

(2) 수정: _____

(3) 이유: _____

3 다음 〈조건〉에 맞게 주어진 우리말을 바르게 영작하시오. 봉영여중 3학년 최근 기출 응용

〈조건 1〉 간접의문문을 사용할 것
〈조건 2〉 총 10개의 단어로 구성된 문장으로 영작할 것

네가 왜 어젯밤에 늦게까지 TV를 봤는지 나에게 말해 줘.

→ _____

4 주어진 표현을 사용하여 다음 우리말을 총 16단어로 영작하시오.
(관사도 한 단어로 취급할 것) 방배중 3학년 최근 기출 응용

네가 한 장의 종이로 얼마나 많은 종류의 종이 꽃을 만들 수 있는지 궁금하다.

(a piece of, how many kinds, paper, of, with, paper flowers)

→ _____

NEW WORDS

☐ **wonder** 궁금해하다 ☐ **face** 직면하다 ☐ **frightening** 무시무시한

5 〈조건〉에 맞도록 다음 빈칸에 알맞은 간접의문문을 쓰시오. 문산중 3학년 최근 기출 응용

　　〈조건 1〉　그림에 주어진 문장을 이용해서 쓸 것
　　〈조건 2〉　필요한 경우 단어의 형태를 바꾸거나 추가할 것

She asks _____ .

6 다음 대화의 내용을 전달하는 문장을 완성하시오. 오륜중 3학년 최근 기출 응용

　　A　Is Judy good at playing tennis?
　　B　Yes. She has played tennis for a long time.

　　→ Judy has played tennis for a long time. Now I know why _____

_____ .

7 다음 대화를 읽고, 대화의 흐름에 맞도록 빈칸을 채우되 〈조건〉을 충족하여 쓰시오. 계남중 3학년 최근 기출 응용

　　〈조건 1〉　간접의문문을 사용할 것
　　〈조건 2〉　주어진 단어를 모두 활용해야 하며, 필요하면 단어를 추가하거나 어형을 변화시킬 것

　　A　How long do we have to go? I'm hungry.
　　B　We don't have enough money.
　　A　Can you tell me _____ ? (how, money, have)
　　B　We have only 2 dollars.

8 다음 대화를 읽고, 빈칸에 알맞은 말을 괄호 안의 단어를 활용하여 쓰시오. (필요한 단어를 추가할 것)

> A I met Yuri's parents.
>
> B You did? I wonder _____. (her, what, like)
>
> A They are very nice people.
>
> B Wow, I'd like to meet them.

9 다음 대화의 빈칸에 알맞은 간접의문문을 쓰시오.

> A I want to know _____.
>
> B My new math teacher lives in Sangam-dong.

10 다음 두 문장을 한 문장으로 만들 때 어법에 맞게 쓴 문장은?

> Do you think? What does he want to do now?

① Do you think what he wants to do now?

② Do you think what does he want to do now?

③ What does he want to do you think?

④ What do you think he wants to do now?

⑤ What do you think does he want to do now?

NOW REAL TEST ②

1 다음 우리말을 영어로 옮길 때, 빈칸에 알맞은 간접의문문을 쓰시오.
(주어진 단어를 사용하되 필요한 단어를 추가할 것)

나는 그들이 어제 그것을 샀는지 모른다. (if, bought)

→ I don't know _____ yesterday.

2 다음 중 간접의문문이 <u>잘못</u> 쓰인 문장은?

① I don't know whether she hates cooking.
② Do you know when he finished washing my car?
③ I want to know when can we start.
④ Didn't you know why Molly failed the test?
⑤ She asked me how much homework I had.

3 다음 대화에서 주어진 우리말에 알맞도록 문장을 완성하시오.

A Oh, no. I didn't bring my book again.
B How are you going to study then?
A I'm going to ask the teacher _____. (an extra book)
(그에게 여분의 책이 있는지)

4 다음 글에서 어법상 틀린 부분을 찾아 바르게 고쳐서 글 전체를 다시 쓰시오.

One day, a farmer saw a big egg in the field. He wondered why was the egg in his field. He wanted to know who put the egg there. He asked his wife if did she had put it there, but she said she hadn't done that. He asked his wife again, "Do you think who put it in my field?"

→ _____

_____

_____

NEW WORDS

☐ **hate** 싫어하다   ☐ **fail** (시험에) 떨어지다   ☐ **extra** 여분의   ☐ **field** 밭

- **주의해야 할 조동사 표현**

used to + 동사원형

과거의 규칙적 습관이나 상태 표현 가능. live, be, have 등과 함께 쓰임.

There **used to** be a tall tree near my old house.

내가 전에 살던 집 근처에는 큰 나무 한 그루가 있었다.

would + 동사원형

과거의 불규칙적 습관을 나타냄. 과거의 상태 표현 불가능. live, be, have 등과 함께 쓰지 않음.

There **would** be a tall tree near my old house. (×)

We **would** have lunch together. 우리는 함께 점심을 먹곤 했다.

be used to + -ing : ~하는 데 익숙하다

I **am used to climbing** trees because I used to do that when I was young.

나는 어릴 적에 그러곤 했기 때문에 나무에 올라가는 것에 익숙하다.

had better + 동사원형: ~하는 게 낫다 (부정: had better not + 동사원형)

You look tired. You **had better** get some rest. 너 피곤해 보여. 좀 쉬는 게 낫겠어.

You **had better not** be rude to your uncle again.

넌 삼촌에게 다시는 무례하게 굴지 않는 게 좋을 거야.

확인문제

1 다음 문장과 같은 뜻이 되도록 괄호 안의 단어를 사용하여 문장을 쓰시오.

> Do not water the cactus too often. (had better)

→ _____

2 다음 중 어법상 <u>틀린</u> 문장은?

① You had better stay here longer.

② I used to rest under this tree when I was young.

③ He is used to swimming in the sea because he was raised by the sea.

④ She would live in this town when she was young.

⑤ He would go to the mountain when he was sad.

Chapter

5

접속사

UNIT 09   접속사 that, 등위 접속사

UNIT 10   부사절을 이끄는 접속사

UNIT 09 접속사 that, 등위 접속사

1 명사절을 이끄는 접속사 that

① 주어: **That** he passed the test is unbelievable.

= It is unbelievable **that** he passed the test.
가주어　　　　　　　진주어

② 목적어: I didn't know (**that**) he was my boss.

③ 보어: The truth was **that** she didn't eat anything.

2 so ~ that ... / so that ~

① so ~ that + 주어 + 동사: 너무 ~해서 …하다

He is **so** strong **that** he can lift anything here.

그는 **매우** 힘이 세서 여기 있는 무엇이든 들어올릴 수 있다.

② so that + 주어 + 동사: ~하기 위해

She went to Japan **so that** she could learn Japanese.

그녀는 일본어를 배우**기 위해** 일본으로 갔다.

3 명령문, and/or ~

① 명령문, and ~: …해라, 그러면 ~할 것이다

Remember this, **and** you will get an answer.

= If you remember this, you will get an answer.

이것을 기억**해라, 그러면** 너는 답을 얻을 것이다.

② 명령문, or ~: …해라, 그렇지 않으면 ~할 것이다

Take this map, **or** you will get lost.

= If you don't take this map, you will get lost.

= Unless you take this map, you will get lost.

이 지도를 가지고 가**라, 그렇지 않으면** 너는 길을 잃을 것이다.

She went to Japan so that she could learn Japanese.

PRACTICE

괄호 안의 단어를 사용하여 다음 우리말을 영작하시오. (필요하면 어형을 변화시킬 것)

1 나는 한국에서 인터넷 속도가 아주 빠르다고 생각한다. (think, that, the Internet speed) 개림중 3학년 최근 기출 응용

_____

2 그 불은 너무 강해서 그 건물 전체를 태워버릴 수 있다. (so, burn, the whole building) 오륜중 3학년 최근 기출 응용

_____

와동중 3학년 최근 기출 응용

3 그가 그 아이스크림을 다 먹었다는 것은 사실이다. (true, that, eat, all of the ice cream)

_____

상동중 3학년 최근 기출 응용

4 쉽게 약속을 깨라, 그러면 너는 친구들을 잃을 것이다. (break your promises, easily, and, lose)

_____

NOW REAL TEST ❶

1 다음 두 문장을 한 문장으로 만드시오. <small>양정중 3학년 최근 기출 응용</small>

He is very rich. He can shop every day.

→ He is _____ rich _____ he can shop every day.

<small>발산중 3학년 최근 기출 응용</small>

2 다음 문장과 같은 의미가 되도록 명령문으로 바꾸어 쓰시오. (단, 각 문장에 and나 or를 반드시 사용할 것)

(1) Unless you study English hard, you will not be a global leader.

→ _____

(2) If you forgive others, you will be forgiven someday.

→ _____

3 다음 우리말에 맞게 주어진 단어를 배열하여 문장을 완성하시오. <small>반송중 3학년 최근 기출 응용</small>

그 회사는 더 많은 제품을 생산하기 위해 더 많은 기계를 구입했다.

(products, more, produce, machines, would, more, so that, it)

→ The company bought _____ .

4 다음 문장과 뜻이 같도록 〈조건〉에 맞게 문장을 완성하시오. <small>덕산중 3학년 최근 기출 응용</small>

〈조건〉 and 또는 or를 사용할 것

If you waste paper, more trees will be cut down.

→ Don't waste paper, _____ .

NEW WORDS

☐ **shop** 쇼핑하다   ☐ **global** 세계적인   ☐ **forgive** 용서하다   ☐ **someday** 언젠가   ☐ **product** 제품
☐ **produce** 생산하다   ☐ **cut down** 베다

5 다음 우리말을 괄호 안의 단어를 활용하여 <u>10단어</u>의 영어 문장으로 쓰시오. (필요하면 형태를 변형할 것)

그는 늦지 않기 위해서 지하철을 탔다. (so, that, take the subway)

→ _____

6 다음 두 문장을 so ~ that ... 구문을 사용하여 한 문장으로 만드시오.

The table was very messy. She decided to clean it up first.

→ _____

7 다음 글을 읽고, 주어진 단어를 바르게 배열하여 재민(Jaemin)이가 해야 할 일을 쓰시오.

Jaemin wants to talk to his deaf classmate, but he doesn't understand sign language. What does Jaemin have to do?

→ Jaemin has to _____ with his

deaf classmate. (learn, he, sign language, communicate, so, can, that)

8 다음 글을 읽고, 주어진 단어를 사용하여 밑줄 친 우리말을 영어로 옮기시오.

진수와 민수는 오늘 학교에서 다투었다. 진수가 민수의 말을 오해하면서 생긴 일이었다. 선생님께서는 진수에게 다음과 같이 충고하셨다.

Teacher You had better listen to him <u>네가 그를 더 잘 이해하기 위해서.</u>

(so that, understand, better)

→ _____

NEW WORDS

☐ **messy** 지저분한 ☐ **deaf** 청각 장애의, 귀가 들리지 않는 ☐ **sign language** 수화 ☐ **communicate** 의사소통하다

9 다음 밑줄 친 (A)가 뜻하는 것을 두 개의 명령문으로 나타내시오. 일산중 3학년 최근 기출 응용

> In English class, Mr. Jang wrote a sentence on the board, "No pain, no gain."
>
> Hyojin　　What does it mean, Mr. Jang?
>
> Mr. Jang　It means (A) "If you don't work hard, you won't succeed in the future."

(1) _____ (and를 사용할 것)

(2) _____ (or를 사용할 것)

10 다음 문장과 비슷한 의미가 되도록 빈칸에 알맞은 말을 쓰시오. 한산중 3학년 최근 기출 응용

If you make some noise, you will wake up the sleeping baby.

→ Don't _____ , _____ you will wake up the sleeping baby.

1 다음 빈칸에 알맞은 말은?

_____ he won the lottery is true.

① When   ② That   ③ If

④ Whether   ⑤ So

2 다음 빈칸에 알맞은 말이 차례대로 짝지어진 것은?

- I looked up the word in the dictionary _____ I could find its meaning.
- I believe _____ I can fly and touch the sky.
- Go straight, _____ you will find the building on your left.

① that – so – and

② so that – so – or

③ so that – that – or

④ that – that – and

⑤ so that – that – and

3 〈조건〉에 맞게 다음 문장을 같은 의미의 다른 문장으로 바꾸어 쓰시오.

〈조건〉 and와 or 중 하나를 꼭 쓸 것

(1) If you stop donating, many poor children won't be able to go to school.

→ _____

(2) If you leave this city, you will regret it.

→ _____

NEW WORDS

□ **win the lottery** 복권에 당첨되다 □ **look up** (단어 등을) 찾아보다 □ **meaning** 의미

4 다음 중 밑줄 친 That[that]의 용법이 나머지와 다른 하나는?

① The problem is that nobody was interested in the results.

② That they have enough food is very important.

③ That man who is next to Minu is my uncle.

④ I think that Suji is very smart.

⑤ That he made this machine by himself is fantastic.

5 다음 우리말을 세 가지 문장으로 표현할 때, 같은 뜻이 되도록 빈칸에 알맞은 말을 쓰시오.

그들은 우승하기 위해서 최선을 다했다.

= They did their best in order to win first prize.

= They did their best so as to win first prize.

= They did their best _____ _____ _____ would win first prize.

UNIT 10

부사절을 이끄는 접속사

1. **시간** when(~할 때), while(~하는 동안), until(~할 때까지), since(~한 이후로), before(~하기 전에), after(~한 후에), as soon as(~하자마자), once(일단 ~하면)
   When he plays soccer, he always wears a red uniform.
   As soon as he woke up, he gave her a wakeup call.

2. **이유** because, since, as(~하기 때문에)
   As she didn't have a driver's license, she couldn't rent a car.

3. **조건** if(만약 ~라면), unless(= if ~ not: ~하지 않는다면), as long as(~하기만 한다면)
   If you do your best, I will buy you a new bike.
   Unless you hand in your report by tomorrow, you can't get an A.
   = If you **don't** hand in your report by tomorrow, you can't get an A.
   You may follow me **as long as** you don't make any problems.

4. **양보** though, although, even though, even if
   (비록 ~일지라도, ~에도 불구하고)
   Although he was tired, he helped his son to do his homework.

5. **대조** while(~하는 반면에)
   Cats are usually not faithful to people **while** dogs are usually faithful.
   개는 일반적으로 충직한 **반면에** 고양이는 대개 사람들에게 충직하지 않다.

When he plays soccer, he always wears red uniform.

PRACTICE

괄호 안의 단어를 사용하여 다음 우리말을 영작하시오. (필요하면 어형을 변화시킬 것)

1. 이 티셔츠가 너무 커서 나는 그것을 교환하고 싶다. (exchange, T-shirt, want, because, big) 안용중 3학년 최근 기출 응용

   _____

2. Maggie는 비록 눈이 보이지 않지만 그의 사랑을 느낄 수 있다. (although, blind, feel) 부곡중 3학년 최근 기출 응용

   _____

3. 그가 그 책을 다 읽은 후에 내가 그 책을 빌릴 것이다. (after, finish, read, borrow, it) 감정중 3학년 최근 기출 응용

   _____

4. 시영(Siyeong)이는 매우 친절하기 때문에 많은 사람들이 그녀를 좋아한다. (kind, since) 동덕여중 3학년 최근 기출 응용

   _____

NOW **REAL TEST** ①

1 다음 두 문장을 한 문장으로 만드시오.
(단, '~에도 불구하고'의 의미를 갖는 접속사를 사용할 것) 경서중 3학년 최근 기출 응용

Their house was old and small. But they were happy there.

→ _____

원촌중 3학년 최근 기출 응용

2 '비록 ~일지라도'라는 뜻의 접속사를 사용하여 다음 〈조건〉에 맞게 문장을 완성하시오.

〈조건 1〉 다음 의미가 포함되도록 할 것
  • Harry는 매우 영리하다.
  • 그는 스스로 무언가를 결정할(decide) 수 없다.

〈조건 2〉 빈칸 하나에 한 단어씩만 쓸 것

→ _____ _____ Harry _____ very smart, he _____ _____

anything by himself.

3 다음 우리말을 〈조건〉에 맞게 영작하시오. 영파여중 3학년 최근 기출 응용

〈조건 1〉 There를 활용할 것
〈조건 2〉 10단어로 쓸 것
비록 나의 삼촌 집에는 좋은 책이 많이 있었지만, 나는 솔직히 거기 가고 싶지 않았다.

→ _____, I honestly didn't

want to go there.

4 적절한 접속사를 사용하여 다음 두 문장을 한 문장으로 만드시오. 오주중 3학년 최근 기출 응용

He didn't get enough sleep last night. He needs to take a nap now.

→ _____

NEW WORDS

☐ **honestly** 솔직히

5 다음 중 빈칸에 적절하지 <u>않은</u> 것을 <u>모두</u> 고르시오. 가락중 3학년 최근 기출 응용

They worried about the results _____ they didn't do their best at the audition.

① because   ② since   ③ unless

④ as   ⑤ even though

덕현중 3학년 최근 기출 응용

6 〈A〉와 〈B〉에서 의미상 서로 짝이 되는 문장을 찾아, 접속사를 사용하여 한 문장으로 만드시오.

A   • Many people like Jinyeong's acting in the drama.

      • Nobody thinks badly of him.

B   • He is a rookie.

      • He helps many poor people.

(1) Many people _____.

(2) Nobody _____.

7 빈칸에 공통으로 들어갈 말을 <u>한</u> 단어로 쓰시오. 덕정중 3학년 최근 기출 응용

• Usain Bolt is the fastest man in the world. _____ my father is very fast, he can't run faster than Usain Bolt.

• She donates a lot of money to the poor _____ she is not rich.

NEW WORDS

☐ **worry** 걱정하다   ☐ **audition** 오디션   ☐ **acting** 연기   ☐ **think badly of** ~에 대해 나쁘게 생각하다
☐ **rookie** 신인

8 다음 밑줄 친 (A)를 〈조건〉에 맞게 영어로 쓰시오. 이수중 3학년 최근 기출 응용

〈보기〉 since, a foreign language, they, be, force, at that time, use, to

〈조건 1〉 〈보기〉의 단어를 한 번씩 모두 사용하되, 필요하면 형태를 바꿀 것

〈조건 2〉 완전한 문장으로 쓸 것

(A) 그 당시 그들은 외국어를 사용하도록 강요받고 있었기 때문에, it was a dangerous idea to use Korean.

→ _____

9 다음 우리말과 일치하도록 괄호 안의 단어를 바르게 배열하시오. 김천중 3학년 최근 기출 응용

그 소녀들은 그 가수를 보자마자 울음을 터뜨렸다.

(saw, the girls, tears, as, the singer, burst into, as, they, soon)

→ _____

10 although를 사용하여 다음 문장을 우리말 해석과 같은 의미로 바꾸시오.
(although로 문장을 시작할 것) 동성중 3학년 최근 기출 응용

(1) Ken had dinner, but he is still hungry. (Ken은 저녁을 먹었음에도 불구하고 여전히 배고프다.)

→ _____

(2) Jane is disappointed, but she is smiling. (Jane은 실망스러움에도 불구하고 웃고 있다.)

→ _____

NEW WORDS

☐ **force** 강요하다 ☐ **burst into tears** 울음을 터뜨리다 ☐ **disappointed** 실망한

NOW REAL TEST ❷

---

1 그림을 보고, 빈칸에 들어갈 수 있는 말을 <u>한 단어로</u> 쓰시오.

→ _____ it was stormy last weekend, they went hiking.

---

2 다음 빈칸 ⓐ와 ⓑ에 들어갈 말이 차례대로 짝지어진 것은?

    Look at the painting here. _____ ⓐ _____ I look at it closely, it looks much more fantastic. _____ ⓑ _____ this painting was painted by an unknown painter, many people think it's a very valuable painting.

        ⓐ   ⓑ
① After   –   When
② When   –   Though
③ Though   –   As
④ When   –   Because
⑤ Because –   As

---

3 다음 중 밑줄 친 While[while]의 의미가 <u>다른</u> 하나는?

① He washed the dishes <u>while</u> she was watching TV.
② British people like soccer <u>while</u> Americans like baseball.
③ <u>While</u> you were sleeping, the game finished.
④ He can't do anything <u>while</u> his mom stays at home with him.
⑤ <u>While</u> you are writing a letter, I will prepare dinner.

---

4   다음 중 밑줄 친 Since[since]의 의미가 <u>다른</u> 하나는?

① I have not been to Japan <u>since</u> 2002.

② I studied very hard <u>since</u> I wanted to pass the exam.

③ <u>Since</u> he likes Jessica, he will do anything for her.

④ I like Korean history <u>since</u> it is very interesting.

⑤ The bird couldn't fly away <u>since</u> its wing was broken.

5   다음 중 의미상 <u>어색한</u> 문장을 모두 고른 것은?

ⓐ I can't go abroad as I have a lot of money.

ⓑ The idol group is very popular although it was made only recently.

ⓒ The United States is a very strong nation though its history is not long.

ⓓ As soon as he woke up late, he was late for the meeting.

ⓔ My brothers like soccer while I don't.

① ⓐ, ⓒ   ② ⓐ, ⓒ, ⓓ   ③ ⓐ, ⓓ

④ ⓑ, ⓔ   ⑤ ⓓ, ⓔ

NEW WORDS

☐ **recently** 최근에   ☐ **nation** 국가

● 헷갈리기 쉬운 접속사 관련 표현

because와 because of

- because + 주어 + 동사: ~하기 때문에
- because of + 명사(구)/대명사/동명사: ~ 때문에

Because he is rich, he can buy a big house.

= **Because of** his richness (= **Because of** his being rich), he can buy a big house.

She could survive **because** her sister helped her.

= She could survive **because of** her sister's help.

though와 despite

- though[although] + 주어 + 동사: 비록 ~하지만, ~함에도 불구하고
- despite[in spite of] + 명사(구): ~에도 불구하고

Though it rained heavily, he drove to Busan.

= **Despite** the heavy rain, he drove to Busan.

= **In spite of** the heavy rain, he drove to Busan.

확인문제

1 주어진 단어를 사용하여 다음 우리말과 일치하도록 빈칸을 채우시오.

> 그녀는 아팠기 때문에 지난 주말에 하이킹을 갈 수 없었다. (sick)

(1) _____ _____ _____ _____, she couldn't go hiking last weekend.

(2) _____ _____ her _____, she couldn't go hiking last weekend.

2 주어진 단어를 사용하여 다음 우리말을 영작하시오.

> 그는 실패했음에도 불구하고 절대 포기하지 않았다. (give up, never)

(1) Although

→ _____

(2) Despite

→ _____

Chapter

6

분사구문

UNIT 11   분사구문의 의미

UNIT 12   주의해야 할 분사구문

UNIT 11

분사구문의 의미

1 **분사구문** 접속사 + 주어 + 동사 → 동사 + -ing

2 **분사구문의 의미**

① 시간: when, while, as, after, as soon as

When I arrived at the store, I found that it was closed.

→ **Arriving** at the store, I found that it was closed.

내가 그 가게에 **도착했을 때**, 나는 가게가 문을 닫은 것을 발견했다.

② 이유: because, since, as

As he is kind, he is popular with his classmates.

→ **Being** kind, he is popular with his classmates.

그는 **친절해서** 반 친구들에게 인기 있다.

③ 조건: if

If you walk in the forest, you will feel comfortable.

→ **Walking** in the forest, you will feel comfortable.

숲에서 **걸으면** 편안하게 느낄 것이다.

④ 동시상황, 연속동작: and, while

My father ate ramen **and** drank a cup of coffee.

→ **Eating** ramen, my father drank a cup of coffee.

아버지는 라면을 **드시고 나서** 커피를 마셨다.

While she was watching a movie, she called her friend.

→ **Watching** a movie, she called her friend.

영화를 **보면서**, 그녀는 친구에게 전화했다.

⑤ 양보의 부사절은 분사구문도 가능하지만 주로 despite나 in spite of를 많이 사용한다.

⑥ 분사구문의 부정은 Not[Never] + -ing를 사용한다.

Watching a movie,
she called her friend.

PRACTICE

괄호 안의 단어를 사용하여 다음 우리말을 영작하시오. (반드시 분사구문을 사용하고, 필요하면 어형을 변화시킬 것)

1 늦게 일어났기 때문에, 나는 통학 버스를 탈 수 없었다. (get up, take, the school bus) 방산중 3학년 최근 기출 응용

_____

2 Susan은 슬프게 울면서 노래를 부르고 있었다. (cry, sadly, sing a song) 수원제일중 3학년 최근 기출 응용

_____

3 진훈(Jinhun)이는 풍선을 든 채로 공놀이를 했다. (carry, balloons, play with a ball) 백마중 3학년 최근 기출 응용

_____

4 아주 어리기 때문에, 그는 혼자서 지하철을 탈 수 없다. (take the subway, by himself) 무원중 3학년 최근 기출 응용

_____

NOW REAL TEST ①

1 분사구문을 사용하여 다음 문장을 다시 쓸 때, 빈칸에 알맞은 단어를 쓰시오. ^{연주중 3학년 최근 기출 응용}

The girl was wearing shorts, so she was bitten by a mosquito.

→ _____ shorts, the girl was bitten by a mosquito.

2 두 문장이 같은 뜻이 되도록 분사구문을 사용하여 문장을 완성하시오. ^{상계제일중 3학년 최근 기출 응용}

Because he was not rich, he lived a simple life.
= _____, he lived a simple life.

3 다음 두 문장의 뜻이 같도록 빈칸에 알맞은 말을 쓰시오. ^{서정중 3학년 최근 기출 응용}

(1) Because he had no money with him, he couldn't take a taxi.

→ _____ no money with him, he couldn't take a taxi.

(2) Being sick, I couldn't go to school.

→ _____ _____ _____ sick, I couldn't go to school.

4 다음 문장의 밑줄 친 부분을 분사구문으로 바르게 고친 것은? ^{충암중 3학년 최근 기출 응용}

Since he got lost, Robert looked at a map on his phone.

① Got lost, Robert looked at a map on his phone.
② Having lost, Robert looked at a map on his phone.
③ Getting lost, Robert looked at a map on his phone.
④ Get lost, Robert looked at a map on his phone.
⑤ Since having lost, Robert looked at a map on his phone.

NEW WORDS

☐ **shorts** 반바지 ☐ **bitten** bite(물다)의 과거분사 ☐ **mosquito** 모기 ☐ **get lost** 길을 잃다

5 다음 그림을 보고, 소미(Somi)가 현재 동시에 하고 있는 일을 분사구문을 사용하여 표현하시오.

→ _____ music, Somi _____ a book.

6 〈보기〉의 단어를 모두 사용하여 분사구문으로 영작하시오. (필요하면 단어의 형태를 바꿀 것)

〈보기〉   have, can, a lot of, win, the quiz contest, knowledge, she

많은 지식을 갖고 있어서 그녀는 그 퀴즈 대회에서 우승할 수 있었다.

→ _____

7 다음 문장을 분사구문을 포함한 문장으로 바꾸어 쓰시오.

(1) As he wasn't hungry, he skipped his meal.

→ _____

(2) When he does his homework, he usually sits on the sofa.

→ _____

8 다음 우리말을 가장 바르게 영어로 표현한 것은? 관악중 3학년 최근 기출 응용

그는 돈이 하나도 없어서 그 책을 살 수 없었다.

① As he had money, he couldn't buy the book.
② Not being having money, he couldn't buy the book.
③ Having not money, he couldn't buy the book.
④ Not had money, he couldn't buy the book.
⑤ Not having any money, he couldn't buy the book.

9 다음 문장의 밑줄 친 부분에서 생략할 수 있는 것을 모두 생략하여 같은 의미의 문장을 쓰시오. (단, 단어의 형태는 바꿀 수 있음) 성내중 3학년 최근 기출 응용

<u>While they worked together on the farm</u>, they got to be closer.

→ _____, they got to be closer.

10 다음 ⓐ~ⓒ의 문장 전환에서 <u>틀린</u> 곳을 찾아 바르게 고치시오. (각 1개) 원당중 3학년 최근 기출 응용

ⓐ As I was sad yesterday, I went to the sea.
  → Having sad yesterday, I went to the sea.
ⓑ Living on the seashore, he cannot swim.
  → If he lives on the seashore, he cannot swim.
ⓒ Singing together, they danced to Big Bang's songs.
  → While we sang together, they danced to Big Bang's songs.

ⓐ _____
ⓑ _____
ⓒ _____

NEW WORDS

☐ **close** 가까운 ☐ **seashore** 해안, 바닷가

1   다음 밑줄 친 부분을 분사구문으로 바꾸어 쓸 때, 빈칸에 알맞은 말을 쓰시오.

As he was in a bad traffic jam, he couldn't help being late.

→ _____ , he couldn't help being late.

2   주어진 문장과 의미가 같도록 분사구문을 포함한 문장을 완성하시오.

(1) When he heard the news, he was surprised.

→ _____ , he was surprised.

(2) After she finishes washing the dishes, she can watch her favorite drama.

→ _____ , she can watch her favorite drama.

3   다음 문장에서 부사절은 분사구문으로, 분사구문은 부사절로 바꾸시오.

(1) While she was studying for an exam, she went out to have some coffee.

→ _____ , she went out to have some coffee.

(2) Not exercising at all, he is getting fatter and fatter.

→ _____ , he is getting fatter and fatter.

4   〈보기〉에서 알맞은 표현을 골라 각 문장을 완성하시오.

〈보기〉   • Not knowing how to operate the washing machine
        • Taking pictures at the zoo
        • Thinking about his mistake

(1) _____ , he couldn't concentrate on the game.

(2) _____ , she couldn't do the laundry.

(3) _____ , they had a great time.

| NEW WORDS |

□ **traffic jam** 교통 체증 □ **surprised** 놀란 □ **operate** 작동하다 □ **washing machine** 세탁기
□ **do the laundry** 빨래하다

UNIT 12 주의해야 할 분사구문

1 **완료형 분사구문(having p.p.)** 부사절의 시제가 주절의 시제보다 앞설 때

After he **had eaten** the chicken, he **watched** TV.
→ **Having eaten** the chicken, he watched TV.

2 **수동형 분사구문**

① 단순 수동: (being) p.p.

When she **was chased** by a dog, she was very shocked.
→ **(Being) chased** by a dog, she was very shocked.

② 완료 수동: (having been) p.p.

After he **had been taught** by David, he could speak English better.
→ **(Having been) taught** by David, he could speak English better.

3 **with + (대)명사 + 분사** '～하면서, ～한 채로'

① 능동: He was running **with his son following**. (현재분사)
② 수동: She thought carefully **with her arms folded**. (과거분사)

Being chased by a dog, she was very shocked.

4 **독립분사구문**

① 분사구문의 주어와 주절의 주어가 서로 다를 경우, 분사구문의 주어를 분사 앞에 쓴다.

Because **Yumi** is very pretty, **many boys** like her.
→ **Yumi being** pretty, many boys like her.

② 분사구문의 관용 표현

Frankly speaking	솔직히 말해서	Judging from	～로 판단하건대
Generally speaking	일반적으로 말해서	Considering (that)	～을 감안하면
Strictly speaking	엄밀히 말해서	Speaking of	～의 이야기가 나와서 말인데

PRACTICE

괄호 안의 단어를 사용하여 다음 우리말을 영작하시오. (필요하면 어형을 변화시킬 것)

1 그녀는 창문이 닫힌 채로 집 청소를 했다. (with, close, clean, windows) 개성중 3학년 최근 기출 응용

_____

2 너의 다리를 올린 채로 누워라. (lie down, legs, with, lift) 마장중 3학년 최근 기출 응용

_____

동산중 3학년 최근 기출 응용
3 기억을 잃어버렸기 때문에, 그는 자기 이름조차 기억하지 못한다. (lose his memory, even, remember)

_____

4 너의 목소리로 판단하건대, 너는 지금 긴장해 있다. (from, voice, nervous) 구월중 3학년 최근 기출 응용

_____

1 다음 우리말을 영작할 때, 빈칸에 알맞은 말을 〈조건〉에 맞게 쓰시오. 귀인중 3학년 최근 기출 응용

〈조건 1〉 주어진 단어를 모두 사용하되 필요하면 형태를 바꿀 것

〈조건 2〉 반드시 빈칸의 수에 맞게 답을 쓸 것

솔직히 말하면, 나는 네가 의미하는 것을 이해하지 못한다. (mean, what, frankly, speak)

→ _____ _____, I don't understand _____ you

_____.

2 〈보기〉와 같이 with를 사용하여 다음 우리말을 영작하시오. 회룡중 3학년 최근 기출 응용

〈보기〉 그는 턱을 손으로 괴고 깊은 생각에 잠겨 있었다.
→ He was deep in thought with his chin resting on his hand.

내 남동생은 머리를 자른 채로 집에 왔다.

→ _____

3 괄호 안의 동사를 사용하여 분사구문을 포함한 문장을 완성하시오.
(단, 필요하면 단어를 어법에 맞게 변형할 것) 회룡중 3학년 최근 기출 응용

(1) 창문이 깨져 있었기 때문에, 우리는 추위를 느꼈다. (break)

→ The window _____, we felt cold.

(2) 네가 숙제를 다 했으므로, 그 만화책을 읽어도 된다. (finish)

→ _____, you may read the comic book.

4 밑줄 친 부분을 분사구문으로 전환할 때, 빈칸에 알맞은 말을 쓰시오. 원미중 3학년 최근 기출 응용

After his computer had been fixed, he started to play the game again.

→ _____, he started to play the game again.

NEW WORDS

☐ **chin** 턱 ☐ **rest** 기대다, 올려 놓다 ☐ **fix** 고치다

5 〈보기〉에 주어진 단어를 바르게 배열하여 우리말 뜻에 알맞은 문장을 완성하시오. 화원중 3학년 최근 기출 응용

〈보기〉 with mud, his boots, with, covered

상우는 진흙으로 범벅이 된 장화를 신고 집에 왔다.

→ Sangu came home _____ .

대림중 3학년 최근 기출 응용

6 괄호 안에 주어진 단어를 다음 우리말에 맞게 배열하시오. (필요하면 단어의 형태를 변화시킬 것)

엄밀히 말해서, 너의 보고서는 더 수정되어야 한다.
(report, strictly, should, your, speak, be, more, revise)

→ _____

7 〈보기〉의 단어를 사용하여 다음 우리말을 분사구문을 포함한 영어 문장으로 바꾸어 쓰시오.
(10단어로 쓸 것, 단어 중복 사용 가능, 형태 변형 가능) 반포중 3학년 최근 기출 응용

〈보기〉 write, to, easy

쉬운 중국어로 쓰여졌기 때문에, 그 책은 읽기 쉽다.

→ _____

8 다음 〈조건〉을 모두 충족시키는 문장을 쓰시오. 삼선중 3학년 최근 기출 응용

〈조건 1〉 아래 두 문장의 의미를 모두 포함하는 한 문장으로 쓸 것
〈조건 2〉 주어진 문장에 틀린 곳이 있으면 수정할 것
〈조건 3〉 with를 사용할 것

Sarah was standing. Her arms were folding.

→ _____

NEW WORDS

□ **mud** 진흙 □ **report** 보고서 □ **strictly** 엄밀히 □ **revise** 수정하다 □ **fold** 접다

9 다음 그림의 상황에 알맞도록, 주어진 단어와 「with + 명사 + 분사」의 형태를 활용하여 문장을 완성하시오. _{선일중 3학년 최근 기출 응용}

(door, close, call, her friend)

→ Sumin is _____ .

10 다음 글을 읽고, 〈조건〉에 맞게 빈칸에 알맞은 말을 쓰시오. _{하안중 3학년 최근 기출 응용}

〈조건1〉 '안전벨트를 맨 채로'라는 의미가 되도록 쓸 것

〈조건2〉 동사 fasten을 사용할 것

When you are traveling on a plane, make sure to remember this. Stay in your seat _____ while the seatbelt sign is on.

NEW WORDS

☐ **make sure** 확실히 하다 ☐ **fasten** 매다, 고정하다 ☐ **seatbelt** 안전벨트 ☐ **on** 켜진

NOW REAL TEST ❷

1 다음 문장을 분사구문을 포함하도록 바꾸어 쓸 때, 빈칸에 알맞은 말을 쓰시오.

Since she failed the bar exam several times, she feels frustrated.

→ _____, she feels frustrated.

2 다음 대화의 내용을 요약할 때, 빈칸에 알맞은 분사구문을 쓰시오.

Tom   How do you know about the secret island?

Jerry   I know about it because I have been there many times before.

→ _____, Jerry knows about the secret island.

3 다음 대화의 빈칸에 알맞은 것은?

A Do you know what Mr. Jo's job is?

B _____ his uniform, he must be a pilot.

① Speaking of   ② Frankly speaking   ③ Generally speaking

④ Strictly speaking   ⑤ Judging from

4 다음 문장에서 생략할 수 있는 부분은?

Having been painted yellow, my car looks very bright.

① Having   ② been   ③ Having been

④ painted   ⑤ 생략할 수 있는 부분 없음

5 다음 문장의 밑줄 친 부분을 분사구문으로 바꾸어 쓰시오.

<u>Because Ms. Page had given us a lot of homework</u>, we couldn't play outside.

→ _____

NEW WORDS

☐ **bar exam** (미국) 변호사 시험   ☐ **frustrated** 좌절한   ☐ **pilot** 조종사

- 의문사 + **to**부정사 = 의문사 + 주어 + **should** + 동사원형

what to ~ : 무엇을 ~할지

I don't know **what to do** next.

= I don't know **what I should do** next.

when to ~ : 언제 ~할지

They told me **when to return**.

= They told me **when I should return**.

which to ~ : 어떤 것을 ~할지

He hasn't decided yet **which car to buy** for his wife.

= He hasn't decided yet **which car he should buy** for his wife.

where to ~ : 어디로 ~할지

She asked me **where to go** for lunch.

= She asked me **where she[we] should go** for lunch.

how to ~ : ~하는 방법, 어떻게 ~할지

I can't remember **how to unlock** this door.

= I can't remember **how I should unlock** this door.

확인 문제

[1–2] 다음 우리말을 두 개의 영어 문장으로 옮길 때, 빈칸에 알맞은 말을 쓰시오.

1 그는 소연(Soyeon)의 생일 선물로 무엇을 사야 할지를 나에게 물었다.

(1) He asked me _____ _____ _____ for Soyeon's birthday.

(2) He asked me _____ _____ _____ _____ for Soyeon's birthday.

2 그 소녀들은 어디에서 주원(Juwon)을 기다려야 할지 몰랐다.

(1) The girls didn't know _____ _____ _____ for Juwon.

(2) The girls didn't know _____ _____ _____ _____ for Juwon.

Chapter

7

가정법

UNIT 13   가정법 과거

UNIT 14   가정법 과거완료

UNIT 13 가정법 과거

1 가정법 과거 현재 사실에 반대되거나 이루어질 수 없는 일을 가정할 때 사용

① 해석: 만약 ~라면 …할 텐데 (현재로 해석)
② 형태: If + 주어 + 동사의 과거형 ~, 주어 + 조동사의 과거형 + 동사원형 …

  *If절의 동사가 be동사일 경우 were만 사용함

  If I **had** a lot of money, I **would buy** a building.
  (= As I don't have a lot of money, I won't buy a building.)
  If I **were** not short, I **could be** a basketball player.
  (= As I am short, I can't be a basketball player.)

2 I wish 가정법 과거 현재 또는 미래에 실현 불가능한 일을 소망할 때 사용

① 해석: ~하면 좋을 텐데
② 형태: I wish (that) + 주어 + 동사의 과거형 ~

  I **wish (that)** earthquakes **didn't occur** on the Earth.
  (= I am sorry (that) earthquakes occur on the Earth.)

3 as if 가정법 과거 현재의 사실과 반대되는 상황을 가정할 때 사용

① 해석: 마치 ~인 것처럼
② 형태: as if + 주어 + 동사의 과거형 ~

  He talks **as if** he **were** an actor. (= In fact, he isn't an actor.)

If I were not short, I could be a basketball player.

4 Without (= But for, If it were not for) 가정법 과거

Without + 명사(구) ~, 주어 + 조동사의 과거형 + 동사원형 …(~이 없다면)
Without the navigation system, we **would get** lost.
*If it were not for는 if를 생략하고 Were it not for로 도치 가능하다.

PRACTICE

괄호 안의 단어를 사용하여 다음 우리말을 가정법 과거 문장으로 영작하시오. (필요하면 어형을 변화시킬 것)

신일중 3학년 최근 기출 응용

1 만일 그가 피아노 연주하는 법을 안다면, 그녀를 위해 연주할 텐데. (if, know, how to, for)

_____

방산중 3학년 최근 기출 응용

2 만약 내가 키가 더 크다면, 배구팀에 합류할 텐데. (if, taller, join, the volleyball team)

_____

국사봉중 3학년 최근 기출 응용

3 만약 내가 아이언맨(Iron Man)이라면 나쁜 사람들을 물리칠 텐데. (if, bad guys, defeat)

_____

고명중 3학년 최근 기출 응용

4 내가 다가오는 시험의 정답을 알면 좋을 텐데. (wish, on, the upcoming exam, the answers)

_____

NOW REAL TEST ①

1 다음 문장을 〈조건〉에 맞게 가정법 과거 문장으로 다시 쓰시오. _{진선여중 3학년 최근 기출 응용}

〈조건〉 괄호 안에 주어진 단어를 반드시 사용할 것

I am sorry that I don't have any siblings. (wish)

→ _____

2 주어진 단어 중 필요한 것만을 사용하여 다음 문장을 영작할 때, 빈칸에 알맞은 말을 쓰시오. _{상동중 3학년 최근 기출 응용}

내가 너라면, 그녀에게 네 모자를 쓰도록 해 줄 텐데.
(I, you, my, your, she, her, hat, am, is, were, if, will, would, let, get, wear, worn, have, had)

→ If I _____, _____.

3 다음 문장을 〈조건〉에 맞게 바꾸어 쓸 때, 빈칸에 알맞은 말을 쓰시오. _{경덕중 3학년 최근 기출 응용}

〈조건 1〉 반드시 가정법 과거로 쓸 것
〈조건 2〉 as를 반드시 사용할 것

In fact, he is not a millionaire.

→ He talks _____.

4 다음 문장과 의미가 같도록 주어진 단어로 시작하는 문장으로 바꾸어 쓰시오. _{경희여중 3학년 최근 기출 응용}

(1) As I am not a good cook, I can't make delicious food for you.

→ If _____, _____.

(2) I am sorry that I can't drive fast.

→ I _____.

NEW WORDS

☐ **sibling** 형제 자매   ☐ **millionaire** 백만장자

5 다음 문장을 가정법 과거 문장으로 바꾸어 쓸 때, 빈칸에 알맞은 말을 쓰시오. 신일중 3학년 최근 기출 응용

(1) I don't have any money, so I can't go shopping.

→ If I _____ _____ _____ , I _____ go shopping.

(2) He isn't careful, so he often falls down.

→ If he _____ _____ , he _____ _____ often _____ down.

6 가정법 과거로의 문장 전환이 <u>잘못된</u> 부분을 바르게 고쳐서 문장 전체를 다시 쓰시오. 금곡중 3학년 최근 기출 응용

(1) I am sorry I can't speak French well. → I wish I can speak French well.

→ _____

(2) As he is sick, he can't play soccer today. → If he isn't sick, he could play soccer today.

→ _____

7 다음 그림을 보고, 〈조건〉에 맞게 현재 사실에 반대되는 가정법 과거 문장을 만드시오. 개원중 3학년 최근 기출 응용

〈조건1〉 If로 시작할 것

〈조건2〉 가정법 과거로 쓸 것

〈조건3〉 주어진 단어를 반드시 사용할 것 (cure, poor people)

→ _____

8 우리말과 같은 뜻이 되도록 영어 문장을 완성하시오. (단, 괄호 안에 주어진 단어를 반드시 사용하되, 필요하면 단어를 변형하거나 중복 사용할 수 있음) _{고창중 3학년 최근 기출 응용}

우리가 거리에서 샤이니(SHINee)를 본다면, 우리와 함께 사진 한 장을 찍자고 요청할 텐데.
(a, in, the, will, ask, them, to)

→ If we _____, _____.

9 밑줄 친 ⓐ~ⓓ를 어법상 올바른 형태로 쓰시오. _{동북중 3학년 최근 기출 응용}

Kim   If Mr. Yi got more pocket money, he ⓐ <u>waste</u> it all on stupid things.

Yi   That's not true. If I ⓑ <u>have</u> more money, I would spend it on a new bike.

Choi   If I ⓒ <u>win</u> a lottery, I would buy an airplane.

Jang   I ⓓ <u>not buy</u> an airplane if I were you. I would buy a helicopter.

ⓐ _____   ⓑ _____

ⓒ _____   ⓓ _____

10 밑줄 친 우리말에 해당하는 영어 표현을 〈조건〉에 맞게 쓰시오. _{숭문중 3학년 최근 기출 응용}

〈조건 1〉 가정법 과거의 형식으로 작성할 것

〈조건 2〉 주어진 단어를 반드시 사용할 것

(1) If I were the president of Korea, I (물가를 내릴 텐데). (reduce, prices)

→ _____

(2) If I were the principal of my school, I (모든 시험을 취소할 텐데). (cancel, exams)

→ _____

NEW WORDS

☐ **pocket money** 용돈 ☐ **president** 대통령 ☐ **reduce** 내리다, 줄이다 ☐ **price** 가격, 물가 ☐ **principal** 교장
☐ **cancel** 취소하다

1 다음 빈칸에 가장 알맞은 것은?

If he _____ an actor, many directors would cast him.

① be   ② was   ③ were   ④ has been   ⑤ been

2 다음 우리말과 같은 뜻이 되도록 영작할 때, 빈칸에 가장 알맞은 것은?

그는 마치 자신이 유명한 가수인 것처럼 말한다.
= He talks _____ a famous singer.

① if he were   ② as if he was   ③ if he had been
④ as if he were   ⑤ but for

3 다음 우리말에 맞도록 '~이 없다면'이라는 의미의 가정법 과거 표현을 빈칸에 쓰시오.

만약 스마트폰이 없다면, 우리는 서로 더 많이 대화할 수 있을 텐데.

(1) _____ smartphones, we would talk to each other more.

(2) _____ smartphones, we would talk to each other more.

(3) _____ _____ _____ smartphones, we
would talk to each other more.

4 다음 표를 보고, 빈칸에 알맞은 말을 쓰시오.

현재 상태	결과
비가 오고 있음	소풍을 가지 못함
숙제가 많음	일찍 잘 수 없음

(1) If it _____ rainy, I _____ go on a picnic.

(2) If I _____ a lot of homework, I _____ go
to bed early.

NEW WORDS

☐ **director** 감독   ☐ **cast** 배역을 맡기다

가정법 과거완료

1 **가정법 과거완료** 과거 사실에 반대되거나 이루어질 수 없는 일을 가정할 때 사용

① 해석: 만약 ~했다면 …했을 텐데(과거로 해석)

② 형태: If + 주어 + had p.p. ~, 주어 + 조동사의 과거형 + have p.p. …

If I **had been** a dentist, I **would have given** my parents a free checkup.

(= As I was not a dentist, I didn't give my parents a free checkup.)

If I **had learned** golf, I **could have played** with them.

(= As I didn't learn golf, I couldn't play with them.)

2 **I wish 가정법 과거완료** 과거에 실현 불가능한 일을 소망할 때 사용

① 해석: ~했다면 좋았을 텐데

② 형태: I wish (that) + 주어 + had p.p. ~

I wish (that) he **hadn't invested** in the property market.

(= I am sorry (that) he invested in the property market.)

Without the coach's help, she couldn't have finished the race.

3 **as if 가정법 과거완료** 과거의 사실과 반대되는 상황을 가정할 때 사용

① 해석: 마치 ~였던 것처럼

② 형태: as if + 주어 + had p.p. ~

The thief acts **as if** he **hadn't stolen** the car. (= In fact, he stole the car.)

4 **Without (= But for, If it had not been for) 가정법 과거완료**

Without + 명사(구) ~, 주어 + 조동사의 과거형 + have p.p. …(~이 없었더라면)

Without the coach's help, she **couldn't have finished** the race.

*If it had not been for는 if를 생략하고 Had it not been for로 도치 가능하다.

PRACTICE

괄호 안의 단어를 사용하여 다음 우리말을 가정법 과거완료 문장으로 영작하시오. (필요하면 어형을 변화시킬 것)

신화중 3학년 최근 기출 응용

1 그녀가 방탄소년단(BTS)의 공연 표를 샀으면 좋았을 텐데. (wish, BTS's concert, a ticket)

_____

2 내가 만약 그녀의 이름을 기억했었더라면 그녀는 실망하지 않았을 텐데. (disappointed) 석천중 3학년 최근 기출 응용

_____

3 그녀는 마치 Eric과 직접 말했던 것처럼 이야기한다. (talk, as, speak, in person) 상도중 3학년 최근 기출 응용

_____

매탄중 3학년 최근 기출 응용

4 그가 힘든 시간을 보내지 않았더라면, 성공할 수 없었을 텐데. (if, have a hard time, succeed)

_____

NOW REAL TEST ①

1 다음 문장을 If를 사용하여 과거 상황을 가정하는 문장으로 완성하시오. _{광명중 3학년 최근 기출 응용}

You didn't exercise regularly, so you couldn't lose weight.

→ If you _____ regularly, you _____ weight.

2 〈보기〉와 같이 주어진 문장을 바꾸어 쓰시오. _{대덕중 3학년 최근 기출 응용}

〈보기〉 She didn't bring her umbrella, so she couldn't go out in the rain.
→ If she had brought her umbrella, she could have gone out in the rain.

We didn't have a car, so we couldn't drive to the beach.

→ If we _____ , _____ .

3 다음 문장을 가정법 과거완료 문장으로 바꾸어 쓸 때, 빈칸에 알맞은 말을 쓰시오. _{해양중 3학년 최근 기출 응용}

(1) In fact, he didn't know any celebrities personally.

→ He talked _____ _____ he _____ _____ some celebrities personally.

(2) I am sorry you didn't find the answer.

→ I wish you _____ _____ the answer.

4 다음 대화를 읽고, 밑줄 친 우리말을 가정법 과거완료 문장으로 쓰시오. _{광덕중 3학년 최근 기출 응용}

A Did you read the book *The Smartest Solution*?
B Sure. It was very interesting. The main character, Steve, was very smart.
A <u>만약 내가 Steve였다면 그 문제를 풀 수 없었을 거야.</u> (If, solve, problem)

→ _____

5 주어진 문장을 if로 시작하는 가정법 문장으로 바꾸어 쓰시오. 중원중 3학년 최근 기출 응용

(1) I didn't know his email address, so I couldn't send him an email.

→ If ＿＿＿＿＿＿＿＿＿＿＿＿＿＿＿＿＿ , ＿＿＿＿＿＿＿＿＿＿＿＿＿＿＿＿＿＿ .

(2) It was windy enough, so they flew the kites in the park.

→ If ＿＿＿＿＿＿＿＿＿＿＿＿＿＿＿＿＿ , ＿＿＿＿＿＿＿＿＿＿＿＿＿＿＿＿＿＿ .

6 다음 대화를 읽고, 밑줄 친 ⓐ와 ⓑ를 가정법으로 쓰시오. 오륜중 3학년 최근 기출 응용

A I heard you bought a new house. How nice!

B Thanks to Jason, I could buy it. He lent me some money.

A That was very generous of him.

B If he ⓐ not lend me the money, I ⓑ not buy the house.

ⓐ ＿＿＿＿＿＿＿＿＿＿＿   ⓑ ＿＿＿＿＿＿＿＿＿＿＿

상계제일중 3학년 최근 기출 응용

7 다음은 한 해의 아쉬움을 쓴 글이다. 글의 흐름에 알맞게 빈칸을 채워 글을 완성하시오.

〈조건〉 get을 사용하되, 필요하면 형태를 변화시킬 것

As I look back on this year, there was only one thing that I regret. I should have studied English harder. If I ＿＿＿＿＿＿＿＿＿＿ harder, I ＿＿＿＿＿＿＿＿＿＿ a better grade.

8 다음 글의 내용과 일치하도록 괄호 안의 단어를 알맞게 고쳐 문장을 다시 쓰시오. 동수원중 3학년 최근 기출 응용

Abraham Lincoln was a great leader. However, he had hard times. He lost many elections before winning the last one. He never gave up. He wanted to make his dream come true. At last, he won the greatest election in 1860.

If Lincoln (give up) after losing elections, he (win) the election in 1860.

→ ＿＿＿＿＿＿＿＿＿＿＿＿＿＿＿＿＿＿＿＿＿＿＿＿＿＿＿＿＿＿＿＿

NEW WORDS

☐ **look back on** ~을 되돌아보다 ☐ **election** 선거

9 다음 글을 읽고, Steve Jobs가 했을 말을 〈조건〉에 맞게 완성하시오. 상도중 3학년 최근 기출 응용

I am Steve Jobs. I invented many useful products since I had creative ideas. I thought differently, so I could be one of the most innovative people in the world.

〈조건 1〉 〈보기〉의 어구를 반드시 활용하되, 필요에 따라 변형하여 사용할 것

〈조건 2〉 과거의 사실에 반대되는 가정의 내용으로 답을 작성할 것

〈보기〉 don't think differently, invent useful products

→ If I _____ , _____ .

NEW WORDS

☐ **useful** 유용한   ☐ **innovative** 혁신적인

NOW REAL TEST ②

1 밑줄 친 부분을 바르게 고친 것은?

If you had helped them, they <u>didn't get</u> into any trouble then.

① don't get   ② would get   ③ wouldn't get

④ would have gotten   ⑤ wouldn't have gotten

2 다음 대화의 빈칸에 들어가기에 <u>어색한</u> 것은?

A How did you find the right place?

B I used the navigation system. _____ the device, I might not have found that place.

① But for   ② If it had not been for   ③ Without

④ Had it not been for   ⑤ If it were not for

3 다음 우리말과 같은 뜻이 되도록 할 때, 빈칸에 알맞은 말이 순서대로 짝지어진 것은?

내가 어젯밤에 일찍 잤더라면, 오늘 아침에 일찍 일어났을 텐데.

= If I _____ early last night, I _____ early this morning.

① went to sleep – got up

② have gone to sleep – would get up

③ had gone to sleep – would get up

④ had gone to sleep – would have gotten up

⑤ have gone to sleep – would have gotten up

4 다음 표를 보고, I wish로 시작하는 문장을 완성하시오.

이름	과거에 대한 아쉬움
Sam	Not working harder
Nick	Not being friendly to others

(1) Sam: I wish _____ when I was younger.

(2) Nick: I wish _____ when I was younger.

NEW WORDS

□ **get into trouble** 곤경에 처하다   □ **then** 그때   □ **navigation** 항해, 항법   □ **device** 장치

- **사역동사: ～하게 하다**

사역동사 + 목적어 + 동사원형: let, make, have, help*

He **let** me **go** out to play.

The teacher **made** us **clean** the classroom.

She **had** her son **stay** in her office.

John **helped** Sean **(to) wash** his car.

*help는 동사원형과 to부정사 모두 올 수 있다.

사역동사 + 목적어 + to부정사: get, help*

She **got** him **to carry** the boxes.

Several people **helped** us **(to) follow** them.

사역동사 + 목적어 + p.p.

목적어가 사물일 때, 사물은 행동의 주체가 될 수 없으므로 수동의 p.p. 사용

He **had** his watch **repaired**.

(시계는 수리를 직접 하는 게 아니고 수리를 받는 것이므로 p.p. 사용)

확인 문제

괄호 안에 주어진 단어를 어법에 맞게 변형하여 빈칸에 쓰시오.

(1) Let me ＿＿＿＿＿＿＿＿ you. (help)

(2) I'll get Andy ＿＿＿＿＿＿＿＿ you a call (give)

(3) The heavy rain made the airplane ＿＿＿＿＿＿＿＿. (delay)

(4) Mr. Rose had his car ＿＿＿＿＿＿＿＿ to the poor. (send)

(5) She helped the old man ＿＿＿＿＿＿＿＿ some books. (carry)

Chapter

8

화법과 일치

UNIT 15   화법(1)

UNIT 16   화법(2), 일치

화법 (1)

1 화법의 종류

① 직접화법: 다른 사람의 말을 따옴표(" ")를 사용하여 그대로 직접 전달하는 방법

② 간접화법: 다른 사람의 말을 전달자의 입장에서 바꾸어서 전달하는 방법

2 평서문의 화법 전환

① 동사: say → say / say to → tell

② 콤마(,)와 따옴표(" ")를 없애고 접속사 that을 쓴다. (that은 생략 가능)

③ that절의 인칭, 시제, 부사(구)는 적절하게 바꾼다. (시제는 주절에 일치시킨다.)

Billy says, "I like to go fishing with my friends."

→ Billy says **(that) he likes** to go fishing with **his** friends.

3 의문문의 화법 전환

① 의문사 없는 의문문: **ask + if[whether] + 주어 + 동사**

Lyn said to us, "Are you tired today?"

→ Lyn **asked us if we were** tired **that day**.

② 의문사 있는 의문문: **ask + 의문사 + 주어 + 동사**

The boy said to me, "Where are you from?"

→ The boy **asked me where I was** from.

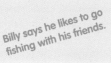

Billy says he likes to go fishing with his friends.

4 화법 전환 시 부사(구)의 변화

this → that / here → there / now → then / ago → before / today → that day / tonight → that night / tomorrow → the next day, the following day / yesterday → the day before, the previous day

The man said to me, "You have to stay here."

→ The man **told me** (that) **I had** to stay **there**.

PRACTICE

다음 직접화법을 간접화법으로 전환하시오.

1 Mr. Kim said, "I don't want to give you a lot of homework." 두일중 3학년 최근 기출 응용

_____

2 She said to him, "You look pale today." 흥덕중 3학년 최근 기출 응용

_____

3 The doctor said to me, "Are you feeling sick now?" 석수중 3학년 최근 기출 응용

_____

4 Tommy said to me, "What do you like to do on weekends?" 매탄중 3학년 최근 기출 응용

_____

NOW REAL TEST ❶

1 주어진 문장을 간접화법으로 바꿀 때, 빈칸에 알맞은 말을 쓰시오. _{중원중 3학년 최근 기출 응용}

Ms. Brown said to me, "You have to submit your report tonight."

→ Ms. Brown _____ me that _____ _____ submit

_____ report _____ _____ .

[2-3] 다음 대화의 내용을 한 문장으로 바꾸어 쓸 때, 빈칸에 알맞은 말을 쓰시오. _{일산동중 3학년 최근 기출 응용}

2

Chloe   I want to buy a new car. I can't decide what to buy.

Tom   I can help you make a choice.

→ Tom told Chloe that _____ .

3

David   Did you send me an email last week?

Julie   Yes, I did.

→ David asked Julie _____ .

4 다음 화법 전환에서 빈칸에 알맞은 말을 <u>모두</u> 고르시오. _{석천중 3학년 최근 기출 응용}

He said to me, "Do you have time to drink some coffee?"
→ He asked me _____ I had time to drink some coffee.

① that   ② if   ③ which   ④ whether   ⑤ since

_{상도중 3학년 최근 기출 응용}

5 다음 우리말과 같은 뜻이 되도록 괄호 안의 단어를 바르게 배열하여 문장을 완성하시오.

그는 나에게 어디에서 과일을 살 수 있는지를 물었다.

(could, buy, where, he, fruit)

→ He asked me _____ .

NEW WORDS

□ **submit** 제출하다   □ **make a choice** 선택하다

6   Tony says, "I collect old stamps."

→ Tony says that _____ old stamps.

① I collected   ② he collected   ③ he collects

④ I collect   ⑤ he has collected

7   Andy said to me, "What kind of movies do you like?"

→ Andy asked me _____ .

① what kind of movies I like   ② what kind of movies do I like

③ what kind of movies you liked   ④ what kind of movies I liked

⑤ what kind of movies did I like

8   다음 글을 읽고, 질문에 답하시오. 산남중 3학년 최근 기출 응용

Angela wanted to become an announcer, but she had a big problem. (A) Her friend Jason said to her, "You are afraid of speaking in public." Angela met the school announcer to get his advice on her nervousness. (B) She told him that she wanted to speak clearly in public.

(1) 윗글의 밑줄 친 (A)를 간접화법으로 바꾸시오.

→ Her friend Jason _____ .

(2) 윗글의 밑줄 친 (B)를 직접화법으로 바꾸시오.

→ She _____ , " _____ ."

NEW WORDS

☐ **announcer** 아나운서   ☐ **be afraid of** ~을 두려워하다   ☐ **in public** 사람들 앞에서   ☐ **advice** 충고, 조언
☐ **nervousness** 소심함, 초조함

9 다음 간접화법 중 <u>틀린</u> 것을 <u>모두</u> 고르시오. _{목동중 3학년 최근 기출 응용}

① The man told me that he had a lot of friends.

② She asked me if I have a new car.

③ The girl asked us where we are from.

④ She told me she was a dentist.

⑤ The boy asked me where was the museum.

10 다음 그림을 보고, 대화의 흐름대로 문장을 완성하시오. _{거원중 3학년 최근 기출 응용}

Princess	Why have you waited for me for 90 days?
Soldier	I wanted to show you my love for you.
Princess	Can you wait for ten more days?
Soldier	Of course.

(1) The princess asked the soldier _____ .

(2) The princess asked the soldier _____ .

1   다음 문장을 간접화법으로 바꾸시오.

Melissa said to Danny, "Where do you want to go now?"

→ Melissa asked Danny _____ .

2   다음 빈칸에 들어갈 말이 차례대로 짝지어진 것은?

Julie told me _____ she had no money. Then, she asked me _____ I had any money.

① that – that   ② that – if   ③ whether – that

④ whether – if   ⑤ if – that

3   다음 문장이 간접화법이면 직접화법으로, 직접화법이면 간접화법으로 바꾸시오.

(1) I asked my dad if I could go abroad to study more.

→ _____

(2) My aunt said to me, "Where did you buy this shampoo?"

→ _____

4   다음 대화를 읽고, 대화의 흐름대로 문장을 완성하시오.

Minseok	Hyemi, why are you late for school so often?
Hyemi	I can't wake up early in the morning.
Minseok	Do you want me to give you a wakeup call every morning?
Hyemi	That would be great. Thanks.

(1) Minseok asked Hyemi _____ .

(2) Minseok asked Hyemi _____ .

NEW WORDS

☐ **wakeup call** 모닝콜

UNIT 16

화법 (2), 일치

The teacher told
us to be quiet.

1 명령문의 화법 전환

① 동사: say, say to → 적절한 의미의 동사로 변환 (tell, order, advise, ask 등)

② 콤마(,)와 따옴표(" ")를 없애고 to부정사(to + 동사원형)로 바꾼다.

*부정 명령문일 경우 'not + to부정사'

The teacher said to us, "Be quiet." → The teacher **told** us **to be** quiet.

2 수의 일치

항상 단수동사를 쓰는 경우	항상 복수동사를 쓰는 경우
• each ~, every ~, -thing, -body, -one	• 쌍으로 이루어진 명사 (chopsticks, glasses, scissors 등)
• -s로 끝나는 과목명, 국가명	• the + 형용사 (= 형용사 + people)
• the number of ~ (~의 수)	• a number of ~ (많은)
• 복수의 숫자를 하나의 단위로 볼 때	
• one of the + 복수명사	

Every child **likes** *Robocar Poli*. / The young **need** to learn from the old.

10 kilometers **is** a long distance for children to walk.

3 시제의 일치

① 주절의 시제가 현재일 때: 종속절에는 어떤 시제라도 가능하다.

② 주절의 시제가 과거일 때: 종속절에는 과거나 과거완료(had p.p.)만 가능하다.

③ 시제 일치의 예외

– 불변의 진리: 항상 현재형으로 쓴다.

– 역사적 사실: 항상 과거형으로 쓴다.

– 제안, 명령, 요구, 주장의 동사(suggest, insist, demand, ask, request, order, propose, require)가 있을 경우: that절에 (should) + 동사원형

The doctor **suggested** that I **(should) exercise** every day.

PRACTICE

괄호 안의 단어를 사용하여 다음 우리말을 영작하시오. (필요하면 어형을 변화시킬 것)

1 그는 나에게 최선을 다하라고 말했다. (tell, do, best) 오주중 3학년 최근 기출 응용

_____

2 선생님은 우리에게 떠들지 말라고 지시하셨다. (order, make any noise) 안용중 3학년 최근 기출 응용

_____

3 모든 일꾼들이 점심으로 돼지고기를 먹기 원한다. (every, worker, for, pork) 잠신중 3학년 최근 기출 응용

_____

4 그 호랑이들의 수는 30이다. (the number of) 모라중 3학년 최근 기출 응용

_____

[1-2] 다음 대화의 내용을 한 문장으로 바꾸어 쓸 때, 빈칸에 알맞은 말을 쓰시오. 원곡중 3학년 최근 기출 응용

1

| Officiator | Be happy forever from now on. |
| Bride and Bridegroom | We will be. |

→ The officiator told the bride and bridegroom _____ .

2

| Clerk | Don't take pictures here. |
| Customer | Okay, I won't. |

→ The clerk told the customer _____ .

3 다음 중 어법상 <u>틀린</u> 문장은? 부곡중 3학년 최근 기출 응용

① A number of monkeys are eating bananas.

② The poor is against the new public policy.

③ The number of banks in my town is more than 10.

④ My mom told me that the Earth is round.

⑤ Economics is hard to understand.

NEW WORDS

☐ **officiator** 주례자 ☐ **bride** 신부 ☐ **bridegroom** 신랑 ☐ **clerk** 직원 ☐ **customer** 고객
☐ **against** ~에 반대하는 ☐ **public** 공공의 ☐ **policy** 정책 ☐ **economics** 경제학

4 빈칸에 알맞은 말이 순서대로 짝지어진 것은? 상경중 3학년 최근 기출 응용

> • A number of deer ＿＿＿＿＿＿＿ running in the field.
> • The number of deer ＿＿＿＿＿＿ 25 today.

① is – was   ② is – are   ③ are – is

④ is – were   ⑤ are – were

5 다음 문장에서 어법상 <u>어색한</u> 곳을 찾아 바르게 고치시오. 양강중 3학년 최근 기출 응용

> The number of traffic accidents have increased in the past two years.

→ ＿＿＿＿＿＿＿＿＿＿＿＿＿＿＿＿＿＿＿＿

6 다음 문장을 간접화법으로 바꿀 때, 빈칸에 알맞은 것은? 안산중 3학년 최근 기출 응용

> Jenny said to me, "Go to your classroom."
> → Jenny told me ＿＿＿＿＿＿＿＿＿＿＿.

① that she goes to your classroom

② to go to your classroom

③ going to my classroom

④ to go to my classroom

⑤ to be gone to my classroom

7 다음 대화를 읽고, 밑줄 친 부분을 간접화법으로 바꿔 쓰시오. 서초중 3학년 최근 기출 응용

> A What did your coach say to you?
> B <u>He said to me, "Don't eat too much for dinner."</u>

→ ＿＿＿＿＿＿＿＿＿＿＿＿＿＿＿＿＿＿＿＿

NEW WORDS

☐ **traffic accident** 교통사고 ☐ **increase** 증가하다 ☐ **past** 지난

8 다음 중 밑줄 친 부분이 어법상 어색한 것은? _{대천리중 3학년 최근 기출 응용}

① Each girl is ready to sleep.

② A number of dogs are gathering around.

③ Every people wait for his or her turn.

④ The Korean War took place in 1950.

⑤ The sun rises in the east.

9 다음 글에서 어법상 틀린 부분 3개를 찾아 바르게 고쳐 쓰시오. _{비산중 3학년 최근 기출 응용}

One of the most popular singers in Korea are Gummy. A number of my friends at school thinks that she is the best singer in Korea. Every students in my class likes her music. I will listen to Gummy's songs today.

_____ → _____

_____ → _____

_____ → _____

10 다음 글을 읽고, 밑줄 친 ⓐ~ⓒ를 어법에 맞게 고치시오. _{방이중 3학년 최근 기출 응용}

ⓐ Mathematics are a very difficult subject. No students in my class like it. Today, the homeroom teacher said that we ⓑ are going to have a math exam next Wednesday. I think two days ⓒ are not enough to prepare for the exam.

ⓐ _____

ⓑ _____

ⓒ _____

NOW REAL TEST ②

1 다음 직접화법을 간접화법으로 바꾸시오.

(1) Tommy said to his sister, "Don't use my computer."

→ _____

(2) Mrs. Jin said to her husband, "Turn on the TV."

→ _____

2 직접화법은 간접화법으로, 간접화법은 직접화법으로 바꾸시오.

(1) The children said to the old man, "Give us some chocolate."

→ _____

(2) He asked her not to give his son anything.

→ _____

3 다음 대화의 밑줄 친 부분에서 틀린 것을 모두 찾아 바르게 고치시오.

A How many children are there?
B <u>A number of children are 30.</u>

→ _____

4 다음 문장에서 어법상 어색한 곳을 찾아 고쳐서 다시 쓰시오.

(1) I told my brother that the capital of Canada was Ottawa.

→ _____

(2) I believed that Jessie has already finished her homework.

→ _____

NEW WORDS

☐ **capital** 수도

- **It is said that**: ~라고 말해진다

  ① 주절과 that절의 시제가 같을 경우

  People say that he is the best dresser.

  →**It is said that** he **is** the best dresser.

  →He **is said to be** the best dresser. (단순부정사)

  ② 주절의 시제보다 that절의 시제가 앞설 때

  They say that he built this building.

  →**It is said that** he **built** this building.

  →He **is said to have built** this building. (완료부정사)

확인 문제

[1-2] 다음 우리말을 영어로 옮길 때, 빈칸에 알맞은 말을 쓰시오.

1
> 그는 외계인이라고 말해진다.

(1) It is _____ that _____ an alien.

(2) He is _____ _____ an alien.

2
> 그는 젊었을 때 훌륭한 댄서였다고 말해진다.

(1) It is _____ that _____ _____ a great dancer as a young man.

(2) He is _____ _____ _____ _____ a great dancer as a young man.

Chapter

9

강조, 도치, 동격

UNIT 17   강조

UNIT 18   도치와 동격

강조

1 do를 이용한 강조 동사를 강조할 때

do/does/did + 동사원형 ('정말로', '꼭'으로 해석)

I love eating pizza. → I **do love** eating pizza.

She looks beautiful today. → She **does look** beautiful today.

I saw a ghost ten years ago. → I **did see** a ghost ten years ago.

2 It ~ that 강조 구문 …한 것은 바로 ~이다

강조하고자 하는 주어, 목적어, 부사구를 It is[was]와 that 사이에 넣는다.

*동사는 강조할 수 없다.

**강조하는 말이 사람일 경우 that 대신 who를 쓸 수 있다.

Giha met IU at the party last night.

→ **It was Giha that** met IU at the party last night. (주어 강조)

→ **It was IU that** Giha met at the party last night. (목적어 강조)

→ **It was at the party that** Giha met IU last night. (장소 부사구 강조)

→ **It was last night that** Giha met IU at the party. (시간 부사구 강조)

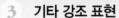

This is the very place that I met her.

3 기타 강조 표현

① the very: 명사를 강조하는 표현으로 '바로 그 ~'라고 해석한다.

This is **the very** place that I met her.

이곳이 내가 그녀를 만난 **바로 그** 장소이다.

② this(이 정도로), that(그 정도로): 형용사나 부사 강조

It hasn't been **this** cold in April since 2007.

2007년 이래로 4월에 **이 정도로** 추웠던 적이 없었다.

Oh, your house is not **that** far.   오, 너의 집은 **그렇게** 멀지 않구나.

PRACTICE

괄호 안의 단어를 사용하여 밑줄 친 부분을 강조하는 문장으로 영작하시오. (필요하면 어형을 변화시킬 것)

청량중 3학년 최근 기출 응용

1   나는 많은 학생들이 버스에서 시끄럽게 얘기하는 것을 <u>정말 들었다</u>. (hear, talk, loudly, on the bus)

_____

2   내가 어제 그녀에게 샌드위치를 <u>정말로 만들어줬다</u>. (make, a sandwich) 관양중 3학년 최근 기출 응용

_____

3   그녀가 오늘 아침으로 먹은 것은 <u>빵</u>이었다. (it, for breakfast) 광무여중 3학년 최근 기출 응용

_____

4   그 건물 앞에서 그 사고가 일어난 것은 <u>어젯밤</u>이었다. (accident, happen, in front of) 관교중 3학년 최근 기출 응용

_____

1 다음 문장에서 밑줄 친 부분이 강조되도록 바꾸어 쓴 문장을 완성하시오. <small>광진중 3학년 최근 기출 응용</small>

Sally cleaned <u>the bathroom</u> yesterday.

→ It _____ .

2 다음 문장에서 밑줄 친 단어를 강조하여 문장을 다시 쓰시오. <small>관교중 3학년 최근 기출 응용</small>

(조건) It ~ that 강조 구문을 사용할 것

Alice made a strong mailbox <u>yesterday</u>.

→ _____

3 주어를 강조하여 다음 문장을 다시 쓰시오. (단, It ~ that 강조 구문을 사용할 것) <small>창포중 3학년 최근 기출 응용</small>

The hunter showed us a rabbit.

→ _____

<small>갈산중 3학년 최근 기출 응용</small>

4 다음 그림을 보고, 진수(Jinsu)가 찾고 있는 것이 무엇인지 It ~ that 강조 구문으로 쓰시오.

Q Is Jinsu looking for a watch?

A No. _____

NEW WORDS

☐ **mailbox** 우편함 ☐ **hunter** 사냥꾼

5 괄호 안에 주어진 단어를 바르게 배열하여 질문에 대한 적절한 답을 쓰시오.
(It ~ that 강조 구문을 사용하고, 필요하면 동사의 형태를 바꿀 것) 삼계중 3학년 최근 기출 응용

    Q When did you visit your uncle?

    A _____

        (my uncle, that, I, be, it, visit, yesterday)

6 It ~ that 강조 구문을 사용하여 다음 질문에 영어로 답하시오. 만수여중 3학년 최근 기출 응용

    Emily bought some food at AW Market this afternoon.

    (1) Who bought some food at AW Market this afternoon?

        → _____

    (2) When did Emily buy some food at AW Market?

        → _____

정의여중 3학년 최근 기출 응용

7 다음 대화 중 밑줄 친 (가)를 영어로 쓰고, 대화의 흐름에 맞게 (나)의 빈칸에 알맞은 한 단어를 쓰시오.

    A Did Ms. Gwon pay for the new glasses?
    B No. (가) 새 안경 값을 지불한 사람은 바로 Ms. Jin이야.
    A Did Ms. Jin really pay for the new glasses?
    B Yes. She _____ (나) _____ pay for them.

  (가) _____

  (나) _____

8 괄호 안의 단어를 강조하여 질문에 알맞은 답을 완성하시오. 초지중 3학년 최근 기출 응용

    (1) Who broke the window yesterday? (Jackson)

        → It _____ .

    (2) Where did she buy this computer? (at a department store)

        → It _____ .

NEW WORDS

☐ **pay for** ~의 값을 지불하다   ☐ **glasses** 안경   ☐ **department store** 백화점

9 다음 대화를 읽고, 빈칸에 알맞은 말을 강조 구문을 사용하여 완성하시오. 중계중 3학년 최근 기출 응용

A　A one-way ticket to Daejeon, please.

B　What time?

A　I want to take the 10:00 KTX.

B　Okay. To Daegu, the 10:00 KTX, right?

A　No, it _____ _____ _____ I want to go to.

B　Oh, sorry. Here it is.

10 다음 대화를 읽고, 밑줄 친 문장을 영어로 쓰시오. (동사를 강조할 것) 문산북중 3학년 최근 기출 응용

Jane　John, I think you don't like me.

John　What are you talking about?

Jane　You didn't send me a present for my birthday.

John　<u>난 너에게 예쁜 가방을 정말로 보냈어.</u>

Jane　Really? Do you know my address?

John　Sure. It's 367 Lord Street, right?

Jane　Oh, no, it's not. It's 365 Lord Street!

→ _____

NEW WORDS

☐ **one-way** 편도의

1 동사를 강조해서 다음 문장을 다시 쓸 때, 빈칸에 알맞은 말을 쓰시오.

(1) She takes good care of her baby sister.

→ She _____ _____ good care of her baby sister.

(2) He called her many times yesterday.

→ He _____ _____ her many times yesterday.

2 다음 대화에서 어법상 <u>어색한</u> 부분을 찾아 바르게 고치시오.

A What did you eat for lunch yesterday? Was it pizza?

B No. That was spaghetti that I ate for lunch yesterday.

_____ → _____

3 판사가 법정에서 누가 범인인지 판결하려고 한다. 그동안 누가 범인인지에 대해 논란이 많았기 때문에 판사는 누가 범인인지를 특별히 강조해서 판결문을 읽으려고 한다. 다음 판결문의 내용을 보고, 판사가 범인을 강조해서 말하도록 빈칸에 알맞은 말을 쓰시오.

Of Jack, Steve, and Leo, Steve stole the car.

→ It _____ that _____ .

4 다음 표를 보고, 괄호 안의 지시에 따라 강조하는 문장을 각각 완성하시오.

선물 상자를 보낸 사람	Tim
선물 상자 안에 있던 물건	a watch
선물 상자를 받은 곳	in my house

A gift box was sent to me from Jeju yesterday.

(1) It was Tim _____ . (보낸 사람을 강조)

(2) It was _____ in the gift box. (받은 물건을 강조)

(3) It was _____ I received the gift box. (받은 장소를 강조)

도치와 동격

1 **부정어의 도치**

① 부정어의 종류: never, hardly, not until, rarely, seldom, little, few, nothing 등

② 일반동사의 도치: 부정어 + do/does/did + 주어 + 동사원형

I never eat ramen after 7 p.m. → **Never do I eat** ramen after 7 p.m.

We hardly imagined that world peace would come so quickly.

→ **Hardly did we imagine** that world peace would come so quickly.

③ be동사의 도치: 부정어 + be동사 + 주어

He is rarely late for school. → **Rarely is he** late for school.

④ 조동사의 도치: 부정어 + 조동사 + 주어 + 동사원형

She could hardly move on the crowded bus.

→ **Hardly could she move** on the crowded bus.

2 **장소 부사구의 도치**

① 어순: 장소 부사구 + 동사 + 주어

The bank is at the corner. → **At the corner is the bank.**

② 주어가 대명사일 경우: 장소 부사구 + 주어(대명사) + 동사

He comes here. → **Here he comes.** (주어가 대명사)

The bus comes here → **Here comes the bus.** (주어가 명사)

3 **동격**

① 명사 + 명사 I have many things to do with **my friend Daniel.**

② 명사 + of + 동명사구

Your hope of eating eight pieces of pizza is stupid.

③ 명사 + that절

The fact that Admiral Yi Sunsin made turtle ships is incredible.

The fact that Admiral Yi Sunsin made turtle ships is incredible.

PRACTICE

괄호 안의 단어를 사용하여 다음 우리말 뜻에 맞게 도치 구문이 되도록 빈칸을 채우시오.

1 결승선 근처에 많은 사람들이 서 있다. (standing)

Near the finish line _____.

2 내가 그녀를 방문했을 때 그녀는 거의 집에 있지 않았다. (at home)

Hardly _____.

3 그는 절대로 컴퓨터 게임을 하지 않는다. (play computer games)

Never _____.

4 학교 버스가 여기 온다. (the school bus)

Here _____.

1 다음 빈칸에 알맞은 것은?

Rooney didn't accept the fact _____ we were not going anywhere on vacation.

① which   ② what   ③ when

④ that   ⑤ of

2 다음 우리말과 같은 뜻이 되도록 괄호 안의 단어를 바르게 배열하여 문장을 완성하시오.

언덕 위에 성 하나가 서 있다.
(a, stands, castle, the, hill)

→ On _____.

3 괄호 안의 단어를 사용하여 두 문장을 한 문장으로 만드시오.

(1) I suggested the idea. My idea was collecting stamps. (of)

→ I suggested _____ collecting stamps.

(2) The belief made me think positively. The belief was that hard work always pays off. (that)

→ The belief _____ hard work always pays off _____

_____ think positively.

4 다음 빈칸에 알맞은 말이 순서대로 짝지어진 것은?

• On the bed _____ sleeping a cat.
• At the library _____ Sam and Lucy every Saturday.

① does – meets   ② was – meet

③ is – meets   ④ does – meet

⑤ was – meeting

5 다음 문장을 hardly를 강조하여 도치시켰을 때 바르게 쓴 것은?

He hardly worked hard when he was here.

① Hardly worked hard he when he was here.
② Hardly he worked hard when he was here.
③ Hardly did he worked hard when he was here.
④ Hardly did he work hard when he was here.
⑤ Hardly he did work hard when he was here.

6 다음 중 밑줄 친 that의 쓰임이 다른 하나는?

① The fact that she is from Germany makes me confused.
② He heard the news that his brother won a gold medal.
③ I have a dream that people around the world will love one another.
④ I bought a new car that is very cool.
⑤ The idea that we can save money sounds realistic.

7 괄호 안의 단어를 바르게 배열하여 우리말과 일치하도록 문장을 완성하시오.

그들은 그렇게 지저분한 식당은 본 적이 없다.
(restaurant, such, dirty, a, seen)

→ Never have _____.

8 다음 문장을 주어진 단어로 시작하는 문장으로 다시 쓰시오.

(1) She never knew that Jake didn't like her.

→ Never _____.

(2) My pet cat rarely goes out without me.

→ Rarely _____.

NEW WORDS

☐ **confused** 혼란스러운, 어리둥절한   ☐ **realistic** 현실적인

9   다음 글의 빈칸에 알맞은 것을 <u>모두</u> 고르시오.

> _____ could I study last night because there were lots of exciting soccer games on TV. I couldn't stop watching TV. Tonight, I will study very hard. I'm going to concentrate on studying.

① Hardly   ② Never   ③ Scarcely

④ Hard   ⑤ Generally

10   다음 그림에 대한 상황 설명을 읽고, 물음에 답하시오.

> Becky will go camping next week. There will be many programs on the day. However, the fact ___ⓐ___ the programs include bungee jumping worries her. Never ___ⓑ___ bungee jumping before. What can she do?

(1) 빈칸 ⓐ에 알맞은 말을 쓰시오.

→ _____

(2) 빈칸 ⓑ에 알맞은 말을 쓰시오. (Becky가 번지점프를 해본 적이 없다는 내용으로 쓰되, 동사 try를 사용할 것)

→ _____

NOW REAL TEST ❷

1 〈보기〉와 같이 문장의 일부를 강조하는 문장으로 쓸 때, 빈칸에 알맞은 말을 쓰시오.

> 〈보기〉 The dogs are on the sofa.
> → On the sofa are the dogs.

(1) An old tree stands on the hill.

→ On the hill _____.

(2) The rain came down.

→ Down _____.

(3) My boss hardly ever sits down when he is working.

→ Hardly ever _____.

2 다음 우리말을 도치 구문으로 영작할 때, 빈칸에 알맞은 말을 쓰시오.

(1) 큰 버스 한 대가 여기로 옵니다.

→ Here _____.

(2) 그녀가 마침내 여기로 옵니다. (finally)

→ Here _____.

3 다음 중 밑줄 친 That[that]의 용법이 〈보기〉와 같은 것은?

> 〈보기〉 The fact that she is a liar is shocking.

① That he made this bookshelf by himself is unbelievable.
② It was our math teacher that fell down on the ground yesterday.
③ We can share the idea that everybody is equal under the law.
④ That may be a serious problem for me.
⑤ I know the man that is standing in front of the bank.

NEW WORDS

☐ **boss** 상사, 사장 ☐ **finally** 마침내 ☐ **liar** 거짓말쟁이 ☐ **shocking** 충격적인 ☐ **bookshelf** 책꽂이
☐ **unbelievable** 믿기 어려운

- **여러 가지 부정 표현**

전체 부정

① no, none, nothing, no one 등

No boys in my class are handsome. 우리 반의 어떤 남자애도 잘생기지 않았다.

② not ~ any

I **don't** have **any** money in my wallet. 내 지갑에는 돈이 하나도 없다.

부분 부정

① 부정어 + all, every, both

Not all soccer players can run fast. 모든 축구 선수들이 빨리 달릴 수 있는 것은 아니다.

② 부정어 + always, necessarily

The rich are **not always** happy. 부자들이 항상 행복한 것은 아니다.

not A until B : B 하고 나서야 비로소 A 하다

I **didn't** know it was already spring **until** the flowers bloomed.

나는 꽃들이 피고 나서야 비로소 벌써 봄이라는 것을 알았다.

*not until을 강조하기 위해 문두로 보내면 뒤에 나오는 문장이 의문문처럼 도치된다.

(Not until + 주어 + 동사 ~, 조동사 + 주어 + 동사원형 …)

Not until she called my name **could I** recognize her.

그녀가 나의 이름을 불러주고 나서야 나는 그녀를 알아볼 수 있었다.

Not until it stopped raining **did we** play tennis.

비가 그치고 나서야 우리는 테니스를 쳤다.

확인 문제

1 주어진 단어를 활용하여 다음 우리말에 맞게 부분 부정을 나타내는 문장을 완성하시오.

> 모든 농구선수들이 다 키가 큰 것은 아니다. (not, all)

→ _____ tall.

2 다음 우리말에 맞게 not until 도치 구문을 만들 때, 빈칸에 알맞은 말을 쓰시오.

> 엄마가 사탕을 주고 나서야 그 여자아이는 울음을 멈췄다.

→ Not until her mother _____ her some candy _____ the girl

_____ crying.